SAINT DOMINGUE

☆ Plantation

MY ODYSSEY

MY ODYSSEY

EXPERIENCES OF A YOUNG REFUGEE
FROM TWO REVOLUTIONS

By a Creole of Saint Domingue

TRANSLATED AND EDITED BY

Althéa de Puech Parham

INTRODUCTION BY

Selden Rodman

LOUISIANA STATE UNIVERSITY PRESS

Contents

Illustrations

Preface

The original of this volume, written in French long-hand, has been in New Orleans since about 1798, among other family papers; but it has only recently come into my possession. I recall only that my father, James Amédée de Puech, described the work as a fascinating account of an ancestor's flight from the revolutions in France and Saint Domingue. He said also that the young author died in the North soon after the events he describes and before the families moved to New Orleans. Though the author refers to himself merely by the initial " P," I deduce that he was an uncle about six generations removed. All members of the family on my paternal side were French Creoles from Saint Domingue, and like numbers of others, left France about 1685, after the Revocation of the Edict of Nantes. These Creole families established sugar, and other, plantations in Saint Domingue, but they often returned to France on visits and sent their children to Paris for their education.

In 1791, during the early days of the French Revolution, the young author, then sixteen years old, and his sister were at school in Paris. Their mother was also in Paris visiting, and they were among those who fled the terrors of that revolution to find asylum in other countries. This group returned to their Saint Domingue home, where, tragically, the terrible insurrection of that island's long drawn-out revolution immediately erupted. The family remained there about two years, and the young man fought in many uprisings, but after the horrible massacre and burning of Cap Français, the family fled to the United States in 1793. The author returned to Saint Domingue in 1794 to fight again for his native land until the defeat of his cause in 1798, when he joined his mother and family in New York. As New Orleans had also been under French rule, the majority of these Creole refugees finally settled here after landing, or staying, elsewhere in the United States.

Only at the instigation of friends and scholars of rare books and belles-lettres have I attempted to edit and translate this old manuscript for publication. As this work is scattered with verse, which also carries the narrative, much of it has needed to be included. I have been able to give but a feeble idea of the poetry's beauty of rhyme and cadence, since I could only translate it in free verse, with the wish to express the essence of its meaning and the desire to capture a spark of its mood.

It seems to me a word of information should be given here as to the correct meaning of the word " Creole," which is frequently both ignorantly and improperly used. A Creole is solely a person of pure French or Spanish blood who was born on a colonial possession of France or Spain—such colonies as were Saint Domingue and Louisiana. Hence the author signs his *Odyssey* as by " A Creole of Saint Domingue." No person of mixed White and Negro blood is a Creole, though he could be properly called a Creole-Negro if he had part French or part Spanish blood and were born on a French or Spanish possession.

This journal has been edited with some abridging and transposing, in order to make the text more continuously chronological and readable. Only a few dates appear in the text, and most individuals are referred to by initials—some of these are historically known, and are identified.

PREFACE

I would like to take this opportunity to express my sincere appreciation and gratitude to Mr. John Cook Wyllie, then Librarian of the Rare Book Department of the University of Virginia, who first brought to my attention the value of this old document as being the only known first-hand account of that place and period, as well as a rare combination of history, belles-lettres, and high adventure; to Mr. Edward Boykin, Mrs. S. V. Lupton, and Mrs. Jules de Launy for their enthusiasm and helpful suggestions; to Miss Katherine Beville, Miss Margaret Martin, and Mrs. Mabel Tally, librarians of the University of Virginia, for their gracious and kind assistance in finding the reference material I wished—all of the above mentioned being residents of Charlotteville, where I started upon the translation of this old manuscript; and, lastly, to my husband, Dr. Duncan Parham and my young son, Duncan de Puech Parham, for their earnest interest and helpfulness in getting this journal ready for publication.

In this volume will be found a very personal as well as historical account of the events which involved a French family during a terrible epoch.

Althéa de Puech Parham

New Orleans, La.
   June, 1959

Introduction

Anyone who has visited that most ravaged of Caribbean countries, the Republic of Haiti, and observed the melancholy contrast between the remains of its eighteenth century magnificence and the sad but proud makeshift of its present poverty, must inevitably have wanted to know how it all came about. Fragmentary accounts exist of the great slave revolt of 1791. But until the discovery of the present manuscript in New Orleans, we have had no report of the early days of the revolution in Saint Domingue by an actual participant—and nothing at all (to the best of my knowledge) from the side of the French planters, masters of what was until then the world's richest colonial possession.

It is fairly clear from his narrative that the anonymous author of this manuscript was born in Saint Domingue in 1775, and had lived there some years as a child before going to France, from which he returned to the colony in 1791. (" I left my country so young that everything was new to me. . . .") His formative years, in any event, were spent in France to which the rich landowners sent their children to be educated. He tells us of his last days of flight from the French Revolution and of taking ship at Bordeaux. We see him disembark at the Colonial capital of Cap Français, where he is swept up almost at once in the storm of the insurrection. Bewildered, but only momentarily dispirited, he escapes with the other refugees after a hopeless resistance to the revolutionary tide. Landing in Baltimore, he records his first impressions of the new American republic. He returns to the colony to fight an unsuccessful delaying action at the entreaty of the Spanish general, Don Garcías de Moreno. Back in the United States we travel here and there with him for the last time.

That not even his name has come down to us, and that his book consists of no more than eight informal but elaborately stylized letters to friends and members of his family, are the strongest proofs of the manuscript's authenticity. No one with half an eye cocked to posterity could possibly have left an account of a cataclysmic social upheaval so cavalier of exact time and place. It would be quite unfair, I should add, to expect a more conventionally coherent sequence from our author. He was *not* writing for publication, nor even primarily to enlighten those to whom he addressed his letters. In fact, the charm of his narrative is in good part attributable to the circumstance that he wrote as personally and informally as he did. His aim was to entertain. And if he entertains us a hundred and seventy years later, as I feel sure the reader will agree he does, he must have succeeded in his more modest aim well indeed.

We are privileged, then, to read the diary of an individual, not a type. A schoolboy, if you like, but a schoolboy who becomes a man, though without ever losing his youthful verve and humor. We progress with him from romantic adventures to tragic ones and finally to the travelogue of a tourist in our own strange new country. Though he writes in that medley of prose and neo-classical verse that had become the fashion in polite eighteenth century society, a fine vein of irony and a sense of proportion save him from becoming pompous.

Which is not to say that our author wasn't a keen observer, or that we have nothing to learn from what he did see. One must admit that it is disturbing, after having formed in the mind's eye a clear picture of a great moment in history, to read an eyewitness account of the same event. It is particularly disturbing if the eyewitness happens to be a very young man without historical perspective himself; someone who, in the poet's phrase, " did not specially want it to happen." Yet the result of such an experience, if we permit the disturbance to teach us anything, must inevitably be to quicken our awareness of the event, give us a personal involvement in it that no reading of the tidied-up histories can contribute, and ultimately a broader perspective of the age's meaning.

What was the situation of Saint Domingue in 1791, just before the outbreak? And what were the events that actually took place during the author's two recorded visits to the embattled island? Because no reader unfamiliar with the historical circumstances could form a clear picture of either on the basis of his narrative, I feel that it will be helpful to establish briefly the sequence of events, relating them wherever possible to the author's movements.

It was during the sixteen years between our author's birth and his return to Saint Domingue that the nightmare of contradictions in the colony became a waking retribution. For the hundred years after the western third of Hispaniola was ceded to France by Spain, following the Treaty of Ryswyck in 1685, the French had occupied the former hideout of the buccaneers, and discontent had simmered. Outbreaks of violence, like the water-pollution conspiracy of Macandel of 1758, had been answered with fearsome reprisals. The more intransigeant among the slaves customarily took to the hills, where, under the leadership of the priests of voodoo (who kept alive both the African religion and the spirit of resistance) periodic raids were made upon the plantations. If our author ever heard of these matters and of the constant threat under which the colonists lived, he gives no indication of it, nor is it part of his account.

During the seventies and eighties Saint Domingue reached the peak of its commercial development. No other colony in the world was so wealthy, so shrewdly administered—or so ripe for disaster. It supplied two-thirds of the overseas trade of France. It produced most of the coffee and sugar for Europe. Its dyestuffs and precious woods were renowned. Relations between the colony and the mother country were becoming strained. The colonial capital, Cap Français (the Cap Haïtien of today) was the most elegant city in the West Indies. Around it were the sugar refineries in the fertile Plaine du Nord. In the lowlands to the west where once there had been a desert, orchards, cultivated fields, and flower gardens flourished with water carried in aqueducts from the distant mountains.

36,000 whites, 28,000 *gens de couleur*, 500,000 black slaves. . . .

The figures almost tell the story. But not quite. The whites, as our author contends, were often benevolent masters; but the point is rather that those who were *not* caused abuses and a consequent resentment among some of the slaves which became the tinder for savage revolt.

As for the Mulattoes, their resentment was if anything greater than that of the slaves because they had more time and freedom in which to exercise it. Since they owned almost a third of the land by 1791, they were all the more humiliated by restrictive racial legislation. Their full rights as French citizens were " guaranteed " by the liberal *Code Noir* of Louis XIV; nonetheless, the reality of their situation between the slaves whom they feared and the masters whom they abominated was intolerable.

It is not surprising, under the circumstances, that the Mulattoes were the first to strike for freedom. When the French Revolution broke out in 1789, the planters of Saint Domingue made two strategic blunders. They tried to pack the republican legislature with their delegates; and they announced in no uncertain terms that should decisions adversely affecting them be made in France, they would ignore them. The answer of the National Assembly in Paris was to proclaim full political rights for the Mulattoes. When nothing was done by the colonial authorities to carry out this new law, the Mulattoes demonstrated in the streets. Their leaders, Ogé and Chavannes, were broken on the wheel. But before the *gens de couleur* could take further action, the unexpected happened. The black slaves revolted.

Between the outbreak of the insurrection on August 20, 1791, and May of 1793 when the author of *My Odyssey* dates his first letter, a great deal happened in both France and Saint Domingue. In Saint Domingue the slaves, under a variety of local chieftains—Boukman, Biassou, Jean-François, Jeannot—succeeded in driving the master class, and such Mulattoes as had not thrown in their lot with the Negroes, into the fortified towns. The majority of the Mulattoes, under their own leaders—Vilatte, Candy, Rigaud—were endeavoring to maintain some independence between the principal contenders. In the south they were beginning to establish a dictatorship of their own—and to re-enslave the Negroes. In France the extremists, spearheaded by the Jacobins, were preparing to take over the Revolution; and one of their Clubs, the so-called Society of the Friends of the Blacks, was openly advocating emancipation. It is these radical orators whom the author so bitterly denounces as armchair " philosophers " and whose converts at Bordeaux told him even before the slaves had revolted : " The Blacks must be the Whites and . . . strut in your place."

The incidents described in the first letter, dated May 1793, took place during the preceding nineteen months. The author arrived at Cap Français on August 18 or 19, 1791. He had some twenty-four hours to observe the status *quo*. He passed through the city and took horse for his family estate at Fort Dauphin (present-day Fort Liberté) where he observed " the dutiful Africans working in cadence." That night he attended a Congo dance (with voodoo overtones) staged by the slaves in his honor. The next day the insurrection broke out. His family fled to the capital and he enlisted in the Creole militia to try to save their plantation. The letter ends with his effort to account for the uprising in terms of subversive propaganda from abroad.

Abroad and in the colony, this was the chain of events. Early in 1791 the moderate revolutionary government of France had decided to send Commissioners to the refractory island. They arrived, perhaps aboard the same ship as the author, on the eve of the rebellion. They devoted most of their efforts to attempting to block a Royalist counter-revolution in Cap Français. Meanwhile in Paris, Robespierre, the Jacobin leader, was enjoying his first triumph. In May of 1792 the news of the Jacobin " Law of April 4 " reached the Cape. This law affirmed that the Mulattoes and free Negroes should have full political rights, and appointed three new Commissioners to enforce it. On September 18 these civil officers arrived at the colonial capital with a Jacobin army to back them. One of the three, Sonthonax, was a fanatical apostle of the new Religion of Reason. Like Robespierre, his master, and like Lenin and Borodin in our time, he was prepared to sacrifice anyone and anything to keep a virtuous theory inviolate. This *enragé* was also unscrupulous. He announced upon landing that " slavery is necessary to the cultivation and prosperity of the colonies; and that it is neither in the principles nor the will of the National Assembly of France to touch these prerogatives of the colonists." Having made this reassuring statement— reassuring to the Royalists, that is—Sonthonax proceeded to organize the poor-whites of the capital into anti-royalist clubs on the Jacobin model. His next step was to send the vacillating Governor back to France, where the Terror guillotined him. Sonthonax next dissolved the colonial assembly, placing in its stead a tribunal consisting of six whites, five Mulattoes, and one free Negro.

On the 17th of October, 1792, Sonthonax provoked a fight between the Royalist regiments and the National Guard which ended in the expulsion of the officers of the former, chief among whom was the aged Desparbes, whose demise is described by the author in Book III. (He calls him Comte d'E.) Book II, incidentally, in which the author describes the destruction of his estates and the confused fighting with mixed Negro-Mulatto guerrillas east of Cap Français, can not be related to any identifiable historical events, though it does describe two of the known slave chieftains.

On March 9, 1793, Sonthonax left Cap Français for St. Marc to help the Mulattoes crush the Royalists in the west. While he was away two important pieces of news reached the capital. Louis XVI had been executed, and war between France and England had broken out. As he made his way back across the Plaine du Nord it must have been clear to the Jacobin proconsul that the time left for decisive action was growing very short. France was ripe for a conservative reaction and the war was bound to shift power to the military. A new general, Galbaud, had in fact been dispatched to Saint Domingue to hold it at any cost against the English. Galbaud's wife was a local Creole and the landowners took renewed hope from this circumstance that their deliverance was at hand. Galbaud was welcomed with enthusiasm. He is the officer to whom our author refers in Book III when he says " Like two evils of whom one must choose the lesser " (the greater being, of course, Sonthonax, who is never referred to in the manuscript by name, but only by the initial " S.") The youth of the Cape lined up on the General's side and the regular troops followed example.

The climactic moment of this phase of the Revolution had now arrived. On June 10 Sonthonax and the other two Civil Commissioners entered the city at the head of their column of Mulatto troops. They demanded that Galbaud recognize their superior authority and return to France. He agreed, reluctantly; but observing, as he was about to weigh anchor, that the Mulattoes were beginning to butcher the Creoles in the streets, he returned with his two thousand soldiers. The furious battle that ensued is well described in *My Odyssey*, but the author's treatment of the denouement is not so clear. Sonthonax, perceiving that the disciplined troops of Galbaud were getting the upper hand and that his cause was lost, played his last card. He opened the gates of the city to the hordes of Blacks beyond the line of fortifications in the Plain. The ferocious ex-slaves poured into the stricken capital, sacked it, and burned it to the ground. Galbaud, hopelessly outnumbered now, retreated to the waterfront. His fleet, bearing 10,000 despairing refugees, including our author, sailed for the United States.

Book III, covering the period of these events, was dated Baltimore, August, 1793; Book IV, dated May of the following year, covers only the author's first visit to the United States. Book V, dated June 1795, and written at Bizoton, a suburb of Port-au-Prince, begins the account of the author's final adventure in Saint Domingue, in the service of the English. What had happened in the meantime?

Sonthonax, following his *ex post facto* Emancipation Proclamation of August 29, 1793, two months after the destruction of Cap Français, found himself trapped between two new and formidable contenders. To the west and south the English had effected landings and were taking full advantage of the disorganized state of France's prize possession. It was to their standard that the more sanguine of the refugee planters now rallied—though not, as the reader is informed by the author in Book V, without misgivings of a patriotic nature.

To the east, on the border of Spanish Santo Domingo, a new star was rising, that of Toussaint L'Ouverture, shortly to become Imperial France's formidable adversary, and the most remarkable man in the annals of the Negro race. Toussaint's name is not mentioned in the present narrative, though he could not have been far distant when the author was witnessing the depredations of Jean-François' soldiers from his vantage-point under the Creole lady's bed at Fort Dauphin.

However that may be, Sonthonax was about to meet his master in boldness and duplicity. The English, with whom our author was now serving in the west, captured

Môle St. Nicholas on September 22, 1793, and Port-au-Prince the following May 30. In April of 1794 Toussaint, who had joined with Biassou and Jean-François in accepting generals' commissions in the Army of Spain, suddenly defected to France. Sonthonax of course welcomed the Negro general in Cap Français with rejoicing, but less than two months after this surprising development the Commissioner was ordered to return to France and stand trial. He sailed on June 12, 1794—just as our author was disembarking a few miles to the east at Fort Dauphin.

The author's second visit to the embattled island, reported in Books V through VIII, coincides in its initial episodes with the events I have just related. The precise reasons why the " Black Auxiliary Army of Spain " fell upon the shipload of returning Creoles is as obscure to us as it was to the author. The Negro commander, Jean-François, is vividly described, but Toussaint, whose corps was probably withheld from this action across the Spanish border, is not mentioned.

Arriving a few days after his almost miraculous escape, at Môle St. Nicholas, the harbor on the northwest tip of the island, the author finds this stronghold already in English hands, joins forces with them at Arcahaye and Port-au-Prince, commands a company during the delaying actions in that part of the country in 1795-96, and leaves Saint Domingue for the last time with the English evacuation of their bridgehead late in 1797.

As for Sonthonax, he returned to Cap Français, after his acquittal before the revolutionary tribunal in 1796, as chairman of a third trio of Civil Commissioners, appointed by the anti-Jacobin Directoire. This time he was completely outwitted by Toussaint, who now ruled the whole island, and shipped back to France for good. The turncoat Jacobin was to have his revenge on the wily Negro general six years later, but ironically only by the grace of that great liquidator of revolutions, Napoleon Bonaparte. However, the French reconquest of Saint Domingue, and their final loss of the colony which followed swiftly, falls outside the scope of *My Odyssey*.

We can read Sonthonax's speeches even now as though we were reading the most banal calls-to-arms in the Marxist weeklies. The type is all too familiar. Hundreds of thousands of words have been written about Toussaint; but no one with a sharp eye or a quick pen ever observed him off guard. He remains an enigma. Millions of words pursue Napoleon from Corsica to St. Helena without endearing him to us; his ego overshadows his personality. Christophe, the great Negro who succeeded Toussaint and built the astonishing fortress that still dominates the Cape, became the victim of his own fear, surviving more as a mountain than a man. Of all the actors in that tremendous drama a hundred-and-seventy years ago perhaps we are now equipped to know best and like most its least consequential, most carefree and genial participant, the anonymous author of this chronicle!

Behind the mask of the eighteenth-century dandy, with his snuff, his epicurean recipes, and his gallantries, the features of a man are always visible. He matures as we journey with him, but even at sixteen his charm is irresistible.

Only when exposed to the horrors of race war, or reflecting bitterly on the theoreticians of equality in France whose writings he blames for the disaster, does the author describe the Negroes in stereotypes. He sees clearly the weakness of the white militia. " Formed by brave young Creoles full of ardor and good will [they were] accustomed to a sheltered life, and having sensitive skin which was protected during the day from the intense heat and allowed a peaceful rest at night, could not long resist the rigors of their new profession." His first description of the slaves at work and at play is almost lyrical. " All the Negroes are by nature poets and musicians!" he exclaims—and as a devotee of the arts, what higher praise can he give?

On the subject of the British and the Americans, the author is acutely perceptive. In fact he is sometimes frank to the point where it still hurts. " It would be easy to live amicably with our British comrades. All that is needed is to drink strictly hard liquor with them each day, and not to contradict when they repeat that the English nation is the greatest in all the world." For their reputed ability to get others to fight their battles for them, he expresses a grudging admiration.

As for us—" A young lady can properly go out with a young man until midnight, and run about everywhere without her mother; but waltz—for shame!" Our propensity for chewing tobacco, fist fights, or stringing out houses along a straight highway and calling it a town, are duly noted. How much has changed? " The Battery . . . can become the most beautiful [promenade] in the world when the Americans have found their taste and become less tenacious with their money." In Philadelphia he observes democracy at work; in Bristol the disease of chain-reading newspapers; in Juliet's Cradle our genius for making Sunday " the saddest day of the week "; and in Trenton the ubiquity of charlatans. Cleanliness in America, he says, is mainly for appearance's sake, but " already public baths are being established in the big cities; the custom of blowing one's nose in the fingers has ceded to that of using a pocket handkerchief; people are beginning to have their teeth attended to by dentists; and they now actually believe that it is not polite to belch in public in such a way as to make the house shake." Even in 1798, it seems, foreigners were saying of us that " gold is the first title of nobility." Nor was our author the last visitor here to remark that " they still try to teach the good people that the fine arts are worthless."

To comment here on the really fine passages of description, humor, and self-revelation would be to anticipate the reader's enjoyment, and perhaps spoil it. But as I indicated at the beginning, it is the refreshing buoyancy of the author's youth that delights most:

> . . . at my age sorrows are not very lasting.

One moment he can be pouring out his anguish over the loss of his estates, and the next hazing a witless recruit or revealing his discovery of a mushroom-bed in mock heroics. The battle-hardened veteran at St. Marc has hardly lamented, in organ-tones worthy of Bernal Díaz, that " this campaign has nothing in particular to distinguish it from others—the enemy routed, comrades killed or wounded, all manner of privations endured," when pouf! he is composing an ode to a Creole lady, begging her mercy for the crime of having inadvertently hit her with a champagne cork.

I must leave to scholars of French poetry, an appraisal of his verse; he himself makes no grandiose claims:

> My Muse follows me in all places;
> Sometimes I laugh with her,
> Sometimes we cry together . . .
> She comforts my sadness
> Or prolongs my happiness.

Suffice to say that the verse flows effortlessly, and in Mrs. Parham's unpretentious rendering is as easy to read as the prose. I like especially the Virgilian celebration of coffee and other exotic fruits—and pursuits—in a land whose beauty and bounty (I surely agree) are as illimitable as they are abused. And when I return to that fabulous land (as I surely shall) my only regret will be that I can never hope to find a travelling companion so gay, so contagiously enthusiastic, and so *alive*, as the anonymous author of this book.

SELDEN RODMAN

Oakland, New Jersey

MY ODYSSEY

" Too busy to correct,
   Too lazy to abridge,
   I abandon exactitude
   To those who rhyme by trade.
   Others make verses after study,
   I make mine so as not to be bored."

... Gresset

Exordium and Invocation

A Greek bard, loved by the gods of verse,
Charmed of yore the curious crowd
In recounting to them the marvelous tale
Of an errant prince among twenty different peoples.
I must narrate, as he, propelled by urgings;
But I have not, as he, great genius.
My carefree book, only by talent is dictated,
And after honoring me in life
Is going to inscribe me to posterity!
But since, alas! the covetous Fates
Gave me so little of their favors,
To amuse myself, I must limit my success;
And avoid a bizarre contrast
By relying upon what means I have for subjects.
Let Homer keep his King of Ithaca,
His Penelope and his Telemachus,
His brilliant deeds, his monsters, and his heroes,
His gods, marine, celestial, and infernal!
Let him go enamored by a great desire for glory
From place to place searching for an audience,
Paying everywhere his expenses with his songs.
I, who well know this century in which we live,
Where one can sing till utter breathlessness
Without finding one meal to come your way;
I, who am unconcerned with the affairs of kings,
Or who desires not to make a single offering
To flatter Fame, that goddess of a hundred voices;
I, yet young, and only a novice poet,
Rhyme for my friends and to pass the time.
In this manner, today, I undertake
An Odyssey in which I am Ulysses.

3

In recitings, loose and uneven,
In varied but in faithful pictures,
In style, gay, languorous or tragic,
In prose, in verse, and even in music,
All at my ease, and much as I desire,
Will I recount, for nothing better to do,
That, which has occurred, or which will occur,
Here, elsewhere, on sea, or on the land.
I do not wish to implore your assistance,
Obstinate masters of the fount of Hippocrene;
It would only be a loss of my time and pains,
As up to now, I have found you deaf to me;
But as one must have a poetic Muse,
Without need to search so high or far,
I have, thank God, mine close by my side.
Come forth at my call, from your humble corner,
O, my snuff-box! Give me succor!
And near you, what matters to me of
Muses, Phoebus, or even Richelet?
How often for one entire hour
Have I chased a fleeting word.
Have I, without result, prayed to all Parnassus
Scanned many books, made many grimaces,
Gnawed at my nails, or pulled my forelocks?
Then, renouncing my vain enterprise,
If from your depths I take a pinch of snuff,
I find it perched upon my finger-tips!
Assist me a thousand times, if must be,
And when in need of that provocative sneeze,
Render to my brain a sudden shock
To waken and sharpen up my wits,
To clarify my sight and lengthen my memory.
Thanks, then, to my snuff-box, am I able to end
My Exordium, and for my long voyages
I have planned my route and needs.

4

So now I leave; or else, will leave,
Tomorrow perhaps, or during the week,
Or in another month, or with the coming season,
Sooner or later, as dictates my fancy;
I can even, fearing the trip,
Not go at all; which will, no doubt, be
Best for me, and especially for my reader.

Book One

ARGUMENT OF BOOK ONE

The author left Paris in 1791, and set out upon a halting trip for Bordeaux by stage-coach. Companions of the journey. Incidents along the route. I embark for Saint Domingue. The flourishing condition of that island at the moment of my arrival. Insurrection of the Negroes and the conflagration of the habitations on the plains of the Cape. Continuous wars against the revolters for nearly a year. Pictures of the Creoles of both sexes and of the inhabitants in general and their manner of living, and the amusements which the country offers. Reflections upon the condition of the Negroes and upon the would-be philanthropists. All this is set forth in a letter addressed to my college friend, the Chevalier du P., whom I left in Paris and who made me promise to recount to him all the particulars of my voyage.

Mon Odyssée

Livre premier.

Tu sais, mon ami, avec quelle répugnance je me décidai à retourner dans ma patrie. J'étais étonné de ne pas trouver en moi ce sentiment inquiet qui porte toujours nos idées vers les lieux où nous avons pris naissance. hélas! de tristes préssentimens semblaient m'annoncer que je ne les reverrais que pour y connaître l'infortune! ils ~~se~~ ~~font~~ ~~que~~ ~~toujours~~ tous ~~~~ réalisés!

Lorsque les évènemens de la révolution me contraignirent de quitter la france, je promis de t'écrire ce que mon Voyage offrirait d'intéressant. Déjà près de deux ans se sont écoulés, et peut-être m'as tu accusé d'indifférence. va, je ne mérite pas ce reproche, je craignais seulement d'ajouter à tes peines le fardeau de celles de ton ami.

Mais, aujourd'hui, contre l'orage
la raison sait me protéger;
tranquile au milieu du naufrage
je vois et brave le danger.
mon cœur qui près de toi s'envole
ne redoute plus ta douleur,
car en apprenant mon malheur
tu sauras que je m'en console.

Cap Français, Saint Domingue

[MAY 1793]

YOU know, my friend, with what repugnance I decided
to return to my native country. I was astonished not to
discover within me that sentiment of impatience which
carries one's thoughts to the place of his birth. Alas!
Sad presentiments seemed to announce to me that I should
only see it to know misfortunes, which were all realized!

When the events of the Revolution compelled me to
leave France, I promised to write you of anything interesting my voyage offered. Now, since nearly two years
have fled, perhaps you have accused me of indifference—
be it so; I do not merit that reproach. I only disliked
adding to your concerns the burdens which have been
those of your friend.

> But, today, against the storm
> Reason knows how to protect me;
> Tranquil amidst the shipwreck
> I see and brave the danger.
> My heart, which flies to your side,
> Is not now afraid to give you pain,
> For in learning of my misfortune
> You will also learn my consolation.

Since when, you will ask, has this mad-cap Creole
known how to make verse, he who so young had to
rely upon himself and never knew anything of Latin or
rhetoric? What do you think, my friend? the idleness of

9

camp life and the maturing of my emotions have made me a poet! I can say like M. Francalen,

> This talent in my head one fine day was discovered,
> And I was eighteen when to me this occurred.

Besides, I assure you, I am not sorry to have just acquired this innocent means of employing my moments of leisure.

> Ignorant, without pretentions,
> With Nature for my guide,
> On my lyre, simple and timid,
> I modulate a few songs.
> Companion sensitive and faithful
> My Muse follows me in all places;
> Sometimes I laugh with her,
> Sometimes we cry together.
> In fields of Mars, as with Cythera,
> In happiness or in sorrow,
> She comforts my sadness
> Or prolongs my happiness.

My friend, after all my explanations, be not surprised if I permit my Muse to mingle harmonies in this account, half sorrowful and half gay, which I write to you. You should remember the sadness of our last farewells. I left, perhaps for always, that Paris which was already the abode of crime, but still that of happiness for a young man of my age and fortune. I was separated from all my pleasant acquaintances, and from you, the companion of my first follies. What melancholy subjects! It was in this state of mind that, at ten o'clock on the darkest of nights, I placed myself in one corner of the coach which was to transport me to Bordeaux.

I heard only the monotonous sound of the heavy wheels. At last that continuing bass was heightened by snoring, in counterpoint, composed of four distinct parts. There were six of us in the coach, so two persons were not sleeping. I was one of them and I soon discovered that the second was seated next to me. I started conversation with her and learned that my neighbor was a young girl of fourteen, whom her mother had just taken out of the convent and was bringing back to Bordeaux.

> I was young, eager for love,
> Impatiently awaiting the break of day
> To diffuse the countryside,
> And assure me whether my companion
> Had features as lovely
> As her sweet voice and gentle manner.
> Ye Gods! I would say at times, tormented with concern.
> Perhaps, she is, alas, as ugly as the Devil.
> Horrid thought! If a malicious trick
> Such as this be played upon me,
> All is over, and I shall die of sorrow.

What discouraged me was that I met her in a coach. I imagined that a pretty young girl should not travel save in a golden carriage. The young person, on her part, did not seem less anxious; she complained, as I did, at the slowness of the night, and at times, with head bent forward, she seemed to watch for the first reflections of the rising sun to reveal my form. At last, she came, that lazy Aurora, came with her soft light to make me perceive a pretty little seductive face, which vied for freshness with the dawn. My first words were, " Oh, how relieved I am!" I blushingly lowered my eyes, then dared for a moment to look into hers—but you know as well as I all the stages of adolescent love. Perhaps you may blame me for seeking out so early such interests for consolation!

11

But could I be indifferent
To an object so full of charms
Who in this happy moment
Challenged me at arms?
The return of the sweet month of May
Has embellished all of Nature.
Already the neighboring birds
Upon the reborn verdure
Rendered homage to tender love.
From the flowers, which had just opened,
The zephyrs carried me their fragrance.
Over the countryside all as yet
Was calm, except my heart.
Titan's cherished spouse
Opened the doors of the Sun
With her vermillion chariot,
Quickening the grand awakening.
A new sensation
Carried this tumult to my senses;
At my side was Beauty
And I was but sixteen.

Memorandum upon Orleans: The domestics of the Silver Lion are very pretty, the actors of the Theatre are wretched, the Bridge is the fashionable promenade, one meets many cripples, and the preserves are excellent. You must admit I do not resemble those nonchalant travelers who remark upon everything but approve of nothing.

The three gentlemen of the coach, tired of being seated for more than twenty-four hours, hired post-horses to ride ahead of the carriage. This gave us a certain air of majesty which was the cause of an amusing incident that day. Tours was awaiting the arrival of the Republican personage who had been made Bishop, and the residents had contributed to the expenses of giving him a suitable reception.

Along the main road, the National Guard lined either side. A crowd of ladies and priests, armed with parasols and eyeglasses, formed the second row, while the rabble formed the third. The municipal officials, surrounded by a band of musicians, stood at the head of the line.

> Phoebus, at the start of his day's career,
> Was drawing open the dark curtains,
> When along the dusty road
> There appeared a coach-and-six.
> At once a loud cry was given:
> " 'Tis he, 'tis he, 'tis he, 'tis he,
> Present arms! Here is his Eminence!"
> One of our three couriers advanced,
> Was questioned, and he answered, " Yes,"
> Then the Mayor ordered silence.
> To witness this new spectacle,
> I placed myself at the carriage door.
> On my head was a large hat
> Which came almost to my eyelids;
> To the role of Divine prelate,
> My brown suit seemed to well-conform;
> An enormous piece of snuff,
> As long as two lengths of my fingers
> Gave them the pious shape
> Of a Bishop's certain pose.
> Upon this sudden apparition
> The crowd was ready to be blessed,
> And knelt to say " Amen."
> A bonfire then was sparkling,
> And while it lighted up the skies,
> They played: " Where can one better be
> Than in the bosom of one's family? "

13

Unfortunately these gentlemen realized their mistake too soon, and overwhelmed me with insults for having caused them to accept the benedictions I had given them. What ingratitude!

You made me promise upon my departure to send you a few details on the beautiful capital of Touraine. I will instruct you therefore: " The Pheasant " is an Inn where one is commodiously lodged and delicately nourished. Upon my faith, this is all I can tell you for the present, since I only stayed in Tours for the duration of one supper and one profound sleep. We left at high noon. There was a change that took place in our society—the four young gentlemen were replaced by—

> An old soldier wandering to Bagnère
> To recuperate from the rigors of camp life,
> Who twenty times for us recited
> To the end his last campaign;
> A grocer, fat, short and peevish,
> Who was busy going everywhere cornering sugar
> And who said triumphantly:
> " If, perchance, we have a war,
> I will, forsooth, have made a good transaction ";
> A Capuchin, more modest merchant,
> Traveled gratis, rich only by his breviary;
> To the devout he gave, for their silver,
> Some orisons which cost him nothing;
> And Nicolette, the dowager actress,
> Who, on leave, was hurrying to Montauban
> To debut as a leading ingénue.

I was the only one upon whom this latter could try her new roles with some hope of success, but I assure you that I showed an exemplary wisdom. And though gossips have accused me of not being as devout as I should, it was, nevertheless, the very reverent Capuchin who conversed with me exclusively until Angoulême; it is true that one seldom meets a monk with manners so agreeable. He knew how to ally the decorum of his holy office with the polite usages of the court and the nobility. The beautiful course of the Loire, the village hewn in the rock, Amboise with its vast stair-way, Chanteloup with its high pagoda—all furnished him with anecdotes as instructive as they were amusing.

At Angoulême as in Tours, I was taken for that which I was not; but this new error flattered me more than did the first. You know that my build is slightly feminine, the sound of my voice fairly light and my hair curly. Some young fellows imagined that I was a woman in disguise. The blush which covered, uncontrollably, my cheeks, still beardless, and the awkward efforts which I made to dissuade them, only served to confirm their doubts. Two or three of my adorers were handsome youths and beset themselves to cajole the fair sex.

> Their glances, their fine flattery
> Amused so much my soul
> And I took with such relish to their attentions
> That soon I thought I was a maid,
> But when I saw the charming subject
> Whom I had pleased so well
> Towards me come so smilingly,
> Without self-flattery at that moment
> I then well knew that I was male.

The rest of my voyage to Bordeaux was of no interest to me, unless it was the chickens of Barbezieux which, judging by the ones I got to know, merited their reputation. As an expert voyager I shall cite for you the puddings of Blois, the prunes of Tours, and the knives of

15

Chattelleraut, precious objects of which I took pains to make ample provision to prove to my friends that I had traveled the world as an observant philosopher.

Six days after our departure from Paris we arrived at Bastide, where we awaited the boat to take us across the Garonne. Here Mme. XX. took me aside to give me a very touching sermon in which, after several reproaches, I heard words that caused a total upheaval in my ideas.

> As I have always heard,
> Love and marriage best harmonize
> When they are kept apart.
> The first, which seems so sweet,
> Is at best a hypocrite,
> Who wishes to destroy with blows
> The other, whose grace she fears.
> Thus I am not tempted
> To join Marriage with her sister,
> For Love is, in truth,
> Too delightful to bury prematurely.

I then faced my situation with courage. I separated from her whom I thought I loved madly, and I was surprised to find that I did not die. The pleasures of Bordeaux, though less brilliant than those of Paris, helped me to accomplish my cure, and I passed my time very pleasantly between high living, the theatre, and the society of the young officers of the regiment of that garrison, of which M. de F., my relative, was then commander.

From the first day of my arrival, I found occasion to become acquainted with everything and everybody connected with our affairs. I went to the theatre and there four young fellows seemed to examine me from head to foot. Thinking they had the intention of ridiculing me, I advanced toward them and demanded haughtily whether they took me for some curious kind of animal. They melted in excuses; they assured me most politely that only the elegance of my clothes surprised them; they admired particularly the new mode of my boots. Correctly surmising that I had just arrived from Paris, they begged my permission to allow their boot-maker to come to my rooms the next day, to rectify their cuts from the new styles of the capital.

> In spite of their youthful tone
> I saw their speech was in good faith
> And I began to change my own;
> Though proud as Hannibal I may have been,
> I thought indeed 'twould foolish be
> To battle over a boot.

These gentlemen kept their word. They sent to me not only their boot-maker, but their tailor as well; I had the glory of setting the styles for all the little rulers of Bordeaux.

M. T., my manager, turned his home topsy-turvy to receive me well. All his household were agog, from his wife to his scullery-boy, all bustled officiously about to serve me. This was the same merchant who later . . . but, before, we were rich. He introduced me into the Society of the city, with whom, I note in parenthesis, I was very bored, as they were speaking then only about Liberty, Equality, and the Rights of Man, etc. These gentlemen, who owed all their fortune to colonial commerce, graciously said in my presence, knowing me well to be among the proprietors of Saint Domingue, that their most sincere wish was to see the overthrow of that island.

> They said to me: " Whereas, my friend,
> You have been master long enough,

Your slave in his turn must be.
That is natural. And should steel
Destroy the entire population
Of these colonists, who play the mighty,
Then the Blacks must be the Whites
And there strut in your place."

About the beginning of July, I was joined by my family. They left Paris six months ahead of me, in order to visit several relatives, who were living in different provinces of France. Their longest stay was in Aunone in Burgundy; and although it was a small town, my sister contrived not to be bored, thanks to several officers of the artillery with whom she had occasion to play some music. Those ladies had just returned from Strasbourg, where they found the old Baron de E. V., our uncle, who was also expecting to emigrate. He seemed to foretell the fate that awaited us in Saint Domingue, and did his best to make my Mother decide to follow him to the Elector of Nesse Reinfeld, who was a friend, and could promise to give me an advantageous position. It would have been perhaps far happier for us to have heeded his counsel; but my Mother would not dare to decide upon such a question without the approval of her husband.

It was on the twentieth day of July, 1791, that I embarked on the ship, *Le Bouillant*, of which Noël was the captain. My tender Mother was there, from whom I had long been separated, and a dear sister from whom I had seldom parted; also two pleasant young ladies whom we were returning to their parents.

We soon lost sight of the sandy coasts of Saintonge, and I could not help sighing or casting a last look upon that country where I had passed the finest days of my life. Notwithstanding all the horrors that were being acted upon its stage, I write mournfully:

> Farewell France, in past days so beautiful,
> Antique abode of Honor;
> Today the cruel retreat
> Of Crime and Sorrow.
> Farewell, people, in the past so tranquil,
> Loyal, lovable, and generous;
> Today, so vile a rabble,
> So wild and meek a herd.
> I flee from your criminal principles,
> The scourge of our virtues and manners,
> From your frightful tortures
> And your persecuting tyrants.
> Alas! may a just Providence
> Soon punish such heinous crimes,
> And may I see once again in France
> A king, happiness and peace.

Thirty days after our departure, we saw at dawn the high mountains of Saint Domingue. A few hours later, we got in sight of our habitation, and we made the usual signal to announce our approach to friends. The young ladies were so delighted, that they wished to fire the cannon, and they acquitted themselves with much courage, placing one hand on the tinder and the other over their eyes. Soon we found ourselves in front of Fort Picolet, which defended the entrance of Cap Français. The pilot came aboard, and we slipped through the Narrows in full sail.

So here I am, my friend, nearly at your antipodes,
Tranquil on the bosom of the port, vast, sure, and comfortable,
Where five hundred buildings of various Nations
Stretch before my eyes their colorful flags;

19

And here am I, contemplating on a scorched shore
For the first time a people with dark faces.

I had at first a poor impression of our capital. The towering hill at the foot of which it is built seemed to leave no space between itself and the sea; and I was agreeably surprised upon disembarking to find myself in a large city, evenly built and very clean. The houses generally are of one story, constructed of stone and ornamented with balconies. Most have gardens or thick trellises shading them from the sun and furnishing a very good Muscat grape.

The Governor's house is a kind of palace; one approaches it by a beautiful avenue of trees, which serves as a promenade for the inhabitants. The barracks are superb and can hold thousands of soldiers. The other public buildings consist of an immense arsenal, well supplied; a hospital for men, run by monks, and another for women, from which you can see the botanical gardens; the Ursuline Convent, where they teach a few young ladies as well as they can; and a large church, officiated over by secular monks. The city is embellished by several public squares, planted with trees and each provided with a fountain which procures its fresh and limpid water from our neighboring mountains. The largest of these squares serves as a parade ground. The one named Clugny is supplied each morning with farm produce for marketing; this comes from places in the environs of the city and principally from Morne-du-Cap, which is covered with country seats and dwellings. From what I could see, and was told, I was sure one should here have an abundance of good living.

> Our cooks were honestly divine,
> The Medoc furnished us our wine
> Rendered more exquisite by its voyage,
> The game was indeed Heavenly,
> All our fruits were the most savoury,
> Mushrooms covered the plain,
> Our fowl was from Maine
> And our truffles were from Perigoux.
> For adherents of Lent
> There grew vegetables in abundance,
> And I believe the Pope himself
> Would have praised our fish.

I left the boat during the business hours and I was surprised at the activity everywhere. The stores bordering the wharf were immense, and filled with precious merchandise. A large population of all countries and colors passed in the streets. On all sides, workmen were ardently busy with all kinds of labor that is essential to a seaport. Some were lowering aboard hogsheads of sugar or kegs of indigo; others were bailing cotton or filling sacks of cocoanuts. Here, were spread out still-wet coffee beans; there were piles of wood-pulp with which to make dye, or men laboriously rolling numerous logs of mahogany. While many carts departed for rural centers filled with wares from Europe, others were coming to discharge the rich products of this country upon the docks, whence they were carried to the waiting vessels.

We passed the day among festivities at Monsieur B's, our representative.

> And towards evening, comfortably seated
> In an elegant and open coach
> Drawn by six galloping horses,
> Accompanied by our many friends,

The complaisant cavalcade
Brought us to our dwelling,
Where our knowing cooks
Had prepared a festive banquet.

The country house of my family is on a sugar plantation, situated between Cap Français and Fort Dauphin,
near a pretty little river and in view of the ocean. Our
habitation is almost in the center of a plain 14 leagues
long by 3 to 5 leagues * wide, and near a gentle slope of
the mountains to the sea. The entire plain is traversed
by an infinite number of little rivers, which overflow after
the rains and are only feeble litttle brooks in the dry
seasons. Wide roads connect the plantations, which resemble little hamlets, because of the large number of
buildings necessary for the making of sugar and housing
of the Negroes. Here Nature presents a strange aspect,
which often agreeably impresses those who arrive from
Europe. I left my country so young that everything was
new to me, and my eyes gorged themselves upon the
spectacle which surrounded me.

The gentle reflections of the late day
Gilded, just then, the mountain tops,
The escaping breezes from the cool groves
Breathed lovingly upon the countryside.
From the orange trees, great white bouquets
Balanced, casting their ambrosial fragrance;
Barring out the nearby road,
The lemon trees crossed their prickly branches;
The eye, without effort, could overlook the fields,
Where flocks moved upon the green carpet.
Here, trained in elegant enclosures,

* A league in France at that time equalled 2.76 miles, so this
property measured 38.64 by 8.28 to 14 miles.

" Thirty days after our departure, we saw at dawn the high mountains of Saint Domingue."

ENTRANCE TO SUGAR PLANTATION

" A thousand trees surrounded it all . . ."

Grown for every taste, were the choicest vegetables;
There, like a sea, was the waving sugar-cane.
Farther on, banana trees formed an arbor,
And from under their mobile roof
I could see the house where I was born, where I will die, no doubt,
If the heavens are favorable to my wishes
Of allowing me to choose my very last hours.
To render a coolness to these lovely places,
Canals bear their imprisoned waters;
A thousand trees surround it all and present to my eyes
Both the fruits of Autumn and the flowers of Spring.
The many buildings and the blazing furnaces,
The variety of crops and their wise supervision,
The dutiful Africans working in cadence,
The rustic wagon creeking beneath its heavy load,
All attest only to abundance and to peace.

How often, from what I have seen, have I been able
to recognize the injustice of those written diatribes, that
were flooding Europe, against the poor planters of Saint
Domingue! What lies! What exaggerated pictures!
What ignorance of the country, the customs, the habits,
and the laws.

During the past months, between the different revolts
and insurrections, I have seen everywhere Negroes who
were fat, well cared for, and happy. I have seen them
many times, about a hundred of them occupied with work
that twenty Europeans could achieve in much less time.
Their cabins appeared sanitary, commodious, and furnished with the necessary utensils for their needs. These
cabins were surrounded with land where they raised pigs
and a variety of fowl; they had me observe their individual gardens, which were perfectly tended and abundantly planted with all the necessary products of our

country. I noticed that the hospital was the finest edifice on each plantation. I was told that a doctor visited them each day and that women looked after the sick. Other women had the care of the children, to bathe, comb, etc. each morning. I often found idle groups, and was told that these were convalescents, nursing mothers, pregnant women, and old people, who were exempt from service. At sunset I heard the bell ring, and noticed that from all directions the workers retired gayly to rest from their labor until the following morning. This same bell recalled the Negroes to the shelter of their cabins when it commenced to rain, and it rains very often here. As for the huge crime of allowing them to go half-nude, I assure you that upon this point I cannot partake in the indignation of the Philosophers, because since I have been in this country

> The simple and light material
> Of which I have formed my costume
> Seems to me at least as heavy as an anvil.
> And although going about while stretched
> At ease in my open carriage,
> Sweat runs freely over my entire body;
> To see my clothes, my skin, my hair,
> One would think I had downed half-a-bottle.
> So I envy, I assure you, the lot of the happy African
> Who, carefree, carries on his back
> Only the robe that Nature gave him.

Thanks to this costume and to the thickness and oiliness of skin, which Providence has wisely given these races of the Torrid Zone, they can prudently brave the heat which would in a short time kill the European. Moreover, I am convinced that if they go uncovered, it is not because they have no clothing at their disposal.

For those who question the discipline under which they live, it is certainly not more rigorous than that which is observed for soldiers and sailors; and when one realizes that thirty thousand whites are in the center of six hundred thousand semi-barbaric Africans, one should not hesitate to say that discipline is necessary.

The young adult Negroes of our plantation, informed of our return, gathered in a crowd before us, and by a thousand bizarre demonstrations testified to the joy they had in seeing us. Having obtained permission to have a *Calinda*, they assembled on the greensward in front of our house. They were in their Sunday clothes—and most of them would not exchange this finery for fifty full bottles. In general, the men were dressed in large white pantaloons over which fell a colored jacket. The women wore rather thin dresses and short aprons; their kinky hair was covered by a Madras headkerchief, beautifully tied; nearly all had on necklaces and earrings, and I saw some wipe their faces with very fine cambric.

At the assigned signal, they separated in a ritual manner and commenced the different amusements of their country.

> Very soon, one of them assumed the role
> Of the Coryphées of old,
> And grave as a school-master,
> Declaimed in raucous voice,
> An incoherent sentence
> Celebrating our safe arrival.
> The others at the same time,
> Half in treble, half in bass,
> Repeated it all in song,
> With added accompaniment
> Of jumps, gestures, and grimaces of the dance.

The African Laÿs *
With a peculiar grace
Played scenes from Lampsaques †
In the exotic manner of their country,
And a band of Congo Vestris **
Whirled to frenzy, as of yore
The possessed ones did cavort
Upon St. Paris' tomb.
To render the affair complete
The minstrels of this fete,
Bizarrely jumped, sat on their heels,
Rolled their eyes, swayed their heads,
Played on their whining banzas
Or on their drums, which they
Struck with the entire arm.

The banza is simply half a gourd, attached to the end of a stick and upon which are stretched four or five strings; it is an African lyre. There is always in these fetes some kind of buffoon, who, from time to time, launches into the middle of the circle and makes sounds and contortions, and emits offensive epithets to those who are around him. You can perceive that a *Calinda* is an opera-ballet-pantomine. This does not equal Armida and Psyché; but because of the novelty of the spectacle, I derived much pleasure from it.

Though all the Negroes are by nature poets and musicians, you can well surmise that they are not Orpheuses or Anacreons. To give you an idea of their spirit, here is a song in Creole patois which they composed, sang,

* A ballerina of the 18th century.
† A playwright of the period.
** Gaétan Vestris (1729-1808), a famous male dancer of the Paris opera.

26

and even danced, to celebrate my arrival and that of my
sister:

Look, here comes the little master! (*chorus*)
He comes to us along with his sister—Look, etc.
They will be as good as their Mother—Look, etc.
Hmm—Look at the way these whites can smile—Look, etc.
And his sister is so pretty too;—Look, etc.
They look sweeter than our fine grapes—Look, etc.
Come all you who are sitting—Look, etc.
Today is the day to dance the Calinda—Look, etc.
When we have finished our dance—Look, etc.
Our master will give us much good food—Look, etc.
And also much good rum—Look, etc.
So that we will have little work tomorrow—Look, etc.

While our panegyrists sang this beautiful production,
the entire company of approximately two hundred jumped
first on one foot and then the other, with appalling contortions and grimaces, and repeated in chorus after each
verse, " Look, here comes the little master," until they
were out of breath.

My voyage has offered you nothing so far but about
agreeable happenings to me; but, Oh, my friend, what
a cruel account I must now make to you! The day
after my arrival, while partaking with my family of the
pleasures of an excellent lunch, a courier arrived to deliver
to my step-father, commander of the district in which
our property is located, a letter full of the most terrifying news. The slaves, enflamed by emissaries sent from
France, had burned the habitations of our neighbors near
the Cape, after assassinating the proprietors without dis-
tinction of age or sex.

Already the insurrection was causing devastation on
all sides, and they feared it would soon reach our place

of habitation. The report of this terrific catastrophe was widely spread. The frightened families among our neighbors met together at our plantation. The men armed to face the storm; the mothers, wives, sisters were lamenting and gathering in all haste a few precious effects. Desolation and fear were painted on all faces. The sky seemed on fire. Guns could be heard from afar and the bells of the plantations were sounding the alarm. The danger increased. The flames at each moment were approaching and enclosing about us. There was no time to lose; we fled. The victims who escaped at sword's point came to swell the number of fugitives, and recounted to us the horrors which they had witnessed. They had seen unbelievable tortures to which they testified. Many women, young, beautiful, and virtuous, perished beneath the infamous caresses of the brigands, amongst the cadavers of their fathers and husbands. Bodies, still palpitating, were dragged through the roads with atrocious acclamations. Young children transfixed upon the points of bayonets were the bleeding flags which followed the troop of cannibals.

These pictures were not exaggerated, and I more than once saw the sorrowful spectacle. Oh, what sensations of pain I was made to go through on this fatal journey, so different from the one of the evening just past. Prostrated by fatigue, we arrived before noon at the pier at Caracol, which was two and a half miles from where we started. There, herded together in boats too narrow for the quantity of fugitives they must receive, burned by the ardent sun, drenched with sweat, perishing with thirst which there was no water to quench, we were transported to the Cape.

There was no sound, movement, or appearance of the

previous peaceable, rich, commercial city. The streets were deserted. At times, however, one saw the brigands pass by in chains on their way to execution, and wounded soldiers who were being taken to the hospital, or fearful people carrying aboard the vessels their most prized possessions. The inhabitants, already bearing arms, were joined by the army which defended the approach of the city; others, locked in their homes, languished in uncertain desolation.

A most anxious night followed that exhausting day; continual alerts kept everyone awake. One feared being slaughtered by one's servants. Couriers arrived with news, at times favorable and at times depressing. One wept for a relative assassinated or exposed to the dangers of a war of extermination. It was possible to calculate by the reflection of the flames which new habitation was being burned. Detachments of defenders went about the streets; sentinels, placed at each corner, called from minute to minute. One heard from afar the rumbling of burning fires and the explosions and whistling of cannon.

I learned the following day that a little army, assembled in haste by the Marquis de Bouvray, was instrumental in the arrest of the progress of the revolters near Rocou, situated several leagues from the Cape. All the inhabitants of the surrounding parishes vied in rendering assistance. I was too interested in seeing this army assume strength, since it could help preserve my properties, not to hasten to join it with what friends I could find. Communications were cut off on land; I embarked in a rowboat with about a dozen young men, and after sunset we started on our journey.

All seemed arranged in agreement with our desires;
The night about us extended its silent protection;

The transient lulls of the winds of night
Left the sea tranquil but for the breath of the zephyrs;
The crescent moon gave its silvery flicker,
Playing on the tides, which made drawings in the sand;
All was repose; only the sound of the agile oar
Disturbed our troubled hearts from out their reveries.
The pirogue, light and docile to direction,
Glided swiftly over the even waves;
We arrived. But, Oh, heaven! To what spectacle of horror!
Long streams of blood reddened the verdure;
There, lying before us, the brigands' horrible symbol
Was to be seen again, of crime and fury;
There, mutilated bodies of no form or color
Attested to crimes at which Nature would cringe;
Here, the foot jostled a myriad fragments
Of still-smoking roofs, of weapons, of banners.
And farther on, the wounded with agony beset,
Crying, by turns, in piety and sacrilege,
Imploring, accusing, or blaspheming Heaven.
Alas! on all sides, Bellona of the cruel heart
Exposed to our eyes this baneful pageant.

To the camp by the sea, the road offered us the same objects and informed us that these places had been the theatre of a terrible combat. The preceding day, the enemy had employed all its efforts to defend the position which we had sought to take; we overcame them, and the camp was littered with the hacked remains of the victims.

I arrived at the break of day, and was at once conducted into the presence of the old general, who had the goodness to place me among his aides. It was in this manner that, within my first twenty-four hours at home, I shouldered my first arms.

We were crushed by this war. One hundred thousand slaves in full revolt and the entire colony of Saint Domingue only defended by two regiments of the regular army. The rest of the troops consisted of militia, formed by brave young Creoles full of ardor and good-will, but who, accustomed to a sheltered life and having sensitive skin, which was protected during the day from the intense heat and allowed a peaceful rest at night, could not long resist the privations and rigors of their new profession.

> Night and day we chased an enemy
> Who never awaited our approach,
> But to harm us, was never found sleeping.
> Each tree, each hole, each piece of rock
> Hid from our unseeing eyes a cowardly assassin,
> Who, if undiscovered, came to pierce our breasts;
> But who fled or begged for mercy
> When we found him face to face.

It was only in ambuscades that our adversary was formidable; in open country one single white could put to rout twenty of these poor wretches, no matter how well armed. One of their chiefs, by name Jeannot, had fancied to come to our camp, with the intention, no doubt, of making an assault. His troop numbered about six thousand men, some nude, some in tatters, and some grotesquely decked in the rich apparel taken from our wardrobes. They were armed with guns, knives, sticks and all the sharp utensils of kitchen and of farm. They had, as artillery, fifteen cannon taken from our villages, where they had served as signals for alarm, and mounted them on carts in guise of gun-carriages. Their musicians made a hideous din beating cauldrons—all this as an accompaniment to the accustomed shriekings of warring Africans.

We were sitting down to dinner when we saw their

31

signal, which is always the burning of some stalks of sugar-cane. Our general, a man of appetite as well as of combat, decided we should continue with our repast, and after giving several orders for the safety of our quarters, sat down to dinner. We were eating heartily until the moment a cannonball passed through the window and carried away, right under our beards, the table and all the plates. The general, infuriated by this mishap, mounted his horse with food still in his mouth, and left camp with six hundred men and four pieces of artillery. Two hours later one could not find a living Negro within a circle of two and a half miles, and the roads were strewn with their bloody remains.

> My friend, you owe this Odyssey of mine
> To a lofty exploit:
> The feeble infant of the Muse,
> Was installed in this hospital
> By a bullet poorly aimed,
> That snatched me from the fiery arms of Mars
> To place me in an apothecary's hands.
> Quiet, idle, and besmeared with unguents,
> I write to you to pass the time away.
> One other consolation I have found
> Among my passing sorrows:
> I owe much in gratitude
> To these sweet and sensitive Creoles,
> Whose fair sex, with us here, as elsewhere,
> Dotingly cares for an arm in a sling.

I will terminate this martial chapter by a character sketch which can give you an idea of the type of people which we have to combat.

I pursued a Negro whose regalia caused me to judge him to be one of the principal chiefs. As I was about to overtake him, he turned around, took aim, but happily for me, could not make his powder fire as it was too damp. I prepared myself to cleave his head with my sword, whereupon he fell to his knees, kissed my boots, and told me, with tears in his eyes, that he was my Mother's godson, that he was present at my birth, and carried me in his arms more than once, and beseeched me not to kill him; that he was a good Negro and that he had always loved the Whites. His manner disarmed me; I dismounted from my horse before having him conducted to camp. However, a soft sound made me quickly turn my head, and I saw the miserable hypocrite, who had recharged his gun, aiming point-blank at my head; being troubled at finding himself discovered, prevented him from aiming accurately, and the bullet went past me. I fell upon him, but he was on guard for my attack; and there we were both acting as if playing Prisoner's Base. I caught my runner at the moment when he was about to slash me and threw him into some weeds. Even then he had the impudence to maintain that *I had not seen correctly*, and that he loved the son of his godmother too much to try to kill him. When he heard himself convicted by a number of soldiers who had just arrived and had witnessed the incident, he changed his tune and told me in his jargon: " Master, I know that is true. It is the Devil who gets inside of this body of mine. I am a good nigger, but against my will the Devil is too strong." His excuse made me laugh despite my anger, and had I been alone, I would certainly have saved him; but the soldiers seized him and bound him to a tree to be shot. When he saw that his fate was sealed, he began to laugh, sing, and joke. At times, however, reviling us in a furious tone, at times jeering at us in mockery. He gave the signal himself and met

33

death without fear or complaint. We found in one of his pockets pamphlets printed in France, filled with commonplaces about the Rights of Man and the Sacred Revolution; in his vest was a large packet of tinder and phosphate of lime. On his chest he had a little sack full of hair, herbs, bits of bone, which they call a fetish; with this, they expect to be sheltered from all danger; and it was, no doubt, because of this amulet, that our man had the intrepidity which the philosophers call Stoicism.

Notwithstanding our victories, conflagrations continued their ravages. Could we have prevented them? One lone lame or wounded Negro was sufficient to reduce to cinders the largest of our habitations. Alas! It is nearly six months since I saw all my own sugar-cane burned and our best Negroes stolen away. Never had a crop promised a finer return, but my revenue went up in smoke, and here I am ruined for several years, for it would be imprudent to let remain those slaves which are left me, in a spot exposed to raiders and revolters. Dependent as we are on the Africans' labor, you can well see how this blow overwhelmed me.

> For a moment I lost my courage
> And cursed, with an aching heart,
> This so inconstant Fortune
> Who took from me her favor.
> But reason finally came to teach me
> To brave my destiny anew;
> And at the approach of sorrow
> His shield came to defend me.
> Less prudent, but much more tender,
> A Divinity of Consolation
> Appeared to render me assistance,
> Uniting the sweet myrtle of my Muse

34

To the ever-bright laurel of War;
In the very heart of my misery,
He accorded me days of happiness
And rendered lighter my pain
By letting me share my hours between them.
You have always envisioned youth
Crowned only with roses of pleasure,
But Fate has, alas! taken from me my all;
Yet, my Divinity stays ever near me
And I can face adversity.

My letter has already been very long, my friend, but before ending it, I want to give you some idea of my compatriots. Do not judge them all from the portrait I will give you. They were transplanted at an early age upon a hemisphere where many lost their native characteristics and took on the virtues and vices of the countries in which they were raised. The Creole is, in general, very lazy, a little vain, prodigal, inconstant, and a libertine; but his faults are redeemed by important qualities which cause him to be loved and esteemed. He is a good friend, sincere, generous, and brave to temerity; he has natural intelligence, taste for the arts, and his hospitality is praised by all who visit our isle. There are none with deformities, since in their childhood no parts of their delicate bodies were constrained in any way.

We are reproached for not excelling in the sciences, as we do in military training and in accomplishments, but I do not believe this to be a fault of intelligence or judgment. Being educated in France far from our parents, we were relinquished to the care of indifferent teachers who allowed our promising abilities to be smothered by indolence and levity, which are all too natural to us. Besides, that idea of riches, which was foolishly allowed

35

to germinate in our young minds, made us negligent of those studies which we imagined were useless to those who had pockets full of money. The dislike shown for our country is another result of our education which we must look for elsewhere. The Creole at twenty goes back to Saint Domingue to take possession of his fortune, and returns promptly to France to dissipate it according to his fancy.

Let us now talk of my beautiful and gentle compatriots. They possess our virtues and our vices with the modifications that belong to their sex. Though indolent, they have lively temperaments and know how to find enough energy to pursue their amusements. They are tall, lithe, and well made; they have a voluptous bearing, their features, irregular but pleasing, seem to have been drawn by Love, but less to inspire great passions than to instill sudden fancies. They have social graces and pleasing talents; they are remarkable above all for their extreme propriety, and those who have never left their isle have an amusing artlessness.

I can only speak to you of the amusements of the Cape as they were. I now know only of the blood-stained games of Bellona and the burning pleasures of the fields of Mars. We previously had a playhouse in which the actors were passable; we had lodges of Freemasons, where large and gay banquets were held; we had a type of literary society for the meeting of delightful and well-informed people.

Often cavalcades were held upon the main roads and barbecues on the plantations which were situated upon rivers. At other times there were musical gatherings, often starting with gambling, and heaven alone knows how the gold and silver rolled. There were endless reciprocal dinners, luncheons, suppers—if one can call these repasts such, which lasted either all afternoon or all night. Those young men who did not care for good society (as one finds this type in all countries) passed their mornings in business and in the public baths, and their nights with mulattresses, who are here the priestesses of Venus.

> But sometimes for variety,
> Filled with desire for combat,
> Armed with a long rapier
> They would go for yea or nay
> To unceremoniously find
> An abdomen or jugular;
> And this was among the pastimes
> Of which they were most fond.

It is hard to have an idea to what point of madness this dueling was carried. Sometimes it was one against one, sometimes two against two, and at others, four against four; there have been seen up to twenty swashbucklers ranged in line on the field of battle, and often the cause was an insignificant bagatelle, at times even fighting for the pleasure alone of fighting.

Here is an example which I could not have believed, if the hero, who is actually a very competent and moderate man, had not told me himself that it was true. One night while trying to keep cool, sitting quietly in front of a colored girl's front door, he found there with him a young Marine officer. The two officers talked amicably, and in the course of the conversation, the Creole remarked that they were having the most wonderful weather. The Marine: " Indeed, yes. There is a delicious coolness."

The Creole: " You must avow, my friend, that no one could desire a more favorable moment to duel."

37

The Marine: " Truly it would be delightful, the coolness, the clearness, and further, the solitude of this street."

The Creole: " Very well, what do you say to our fencing a little? "

The Marine: " Most heartily; I have never refused such a piece of luck."

And here our two Hectors unsheathed and extended strong sword thrusts. Notwithstanding the colored girl's tears and beseechings, she could not succeed in separating them before one had his nose pierced, and the other was slashed in the side.

It must be admitted that there is at all times a ferment of animosity betwen the Creoles and the officers of the Marines. The arrogance and prejudice of the latter can hardly fit together with the same faults that can be found in our own young men.

Just the same, these youths, so turbulent and even so heedless, have, since our trouble, led exemplary lives. No more quarrels, no more duels; their only concern is for their country. And our most fiery young men of the past are today Caesars and Catos.

The manner of life on the plain was quite monotonous; the wealthiest proprietors remained mostly in France. Those whose taste, or the modesty of their revenues, kept them on their properties, lived each according to his fancy. Some saved to retire later in France; others passed their time quietly in the bosom of a large family, and among the decent pleasures and the duties of their state in life.

One word upon our climate. The heat of the sun is extreme, and the country would be uninhabitable if it were not refreshed by the breezes from the sea and from the plain, which arrive regularly each day. We have,

"*The young adult Negroes gathered in a crowd before us. . . . They were in their Sunday clothes. In general, the men were dressed in large white pantoloons over which fell a colored jacket. The women wore rather thin dresses and aprons; their hair was covered by a Madras handkerchief, beautifully tied; nearly all had on necklaces and earrings.*"

NATIVES WASHING CLOTHES

" The heat of the sun is extreme, and the country would be uninhabitable if it were not refreshed by the breezes from the sea and from the plain, which arrive regularly each day."

besides, frequent windstorms which end in hard showers, and these render the nights quite endurable. Then comes what is called winter, when it rains nearly every day. Sometimes there is an entire week when one does not see the sun.

In general, Europeans, upon their arrival, pay tribute to a malignant, but conditioning, fever. They can hope afterwards to enjoy good health, provided that they do not give way to excesses, injurious everywhere, but fatal on the islands. Our doctors understand very well the treatment of this malady, which we call the sickness-of-the-country; however, prevention is more important than the cure, but, in any case, our sick ones cannot be in better care than that of the women of our island, who are attentive, compassionate, and indefatigable on these occasions.

The fair sex is less subject than we to the terrible effects of the climate, but though most of them commence life in perfect health, they retain always a pallor, which succeeds only in adding to their charms.

The temperature of the mountains is very different from that of the plains; and if all new arrivals showed the precaution of remaining in the more elevated region for a few months, they would avoid, no doubt, the necessary danger of becoming acclimated. There, three or four hours of the twenty-four belong to summer; the others are of a pleasant spring. At times, fires are needed in the evening and coverlets at night. Nowhere can one drink a more limpid and pure water. All the vegetables and nearly all the fruits of Europe grow exquisitely and abundantly; the most delicate flowers perfume the air. All told, you see, my friend, Saint Domingue was a country one could inhabit without believing oneself too unhappy:

But, between ourselves, I prefer
Europe and her varied climate.
Here, always there is green upon the earth,
Here, always warm and changeless weather.
Ah, it is monotonous at times;
And bought at too high a price
Are the favors of Latona's son.
How sweet it is after a Winter
To be born again with all Nature,
To see the new, young verdure
Succeed the long white carpet.
Even love is better in Spring;
In Autumn, one hunts and harvests;
And Winter is a gay admixture
Of brilliant arts and pleasures.

Now I will speak to you of the government of the Negroes before the insurrection. I will tell you of the conditions among·these men who have done us so much harm, of these unchained tigers whose roots in barbarism cause Nature to shudder.

You will see how much one must beware of the lying declamations of those egoistic pedants who, from the depths of their libraries, judge everything by hearsay, and make a pretence of feeling compassion for some unfortunates whom they have never seen or known, so they may claim the right to lodge complaint against those people whom they do see daily. If you know any of these gentlemen, remember to tell them that I do not believe as they; theirs is an irremediable crime, and they do not overwhelm me with all the sonorous and high-sounding words of four or five syllables which they can find in the dictionary.

Comfortably dressed in cottons from our isles,
Their houses furnished with our beautiful mahogany,
Treating their delicate tastes
With our coffee and chocolates,
With honey from our delicious roses;
Requesting each day from our happy clime,
Our dyes, our fruits, our drugs, our spices,
And our most humble products.
" No slaves! " they say to us.
There should be none, as who of us is unaware?
But whilst an evil to which we are accustomed,
An evil that extends from princes to subjects,
From our ancestors to us, from West to East,
For an evil whose harm is fraught with blessings,
Their doubtful remedy is cruel in its results.
Is it not better, for the present,
To lament, but endure in peace?
" But no," they coldly cry in fury,
" The African must be free and the master die! "
Which they have done their best to bring about.
Well, compassionate friends of the African races,
Come here and look over our productive plains
Whose treasures, before, were carefully gathered
For commerce to disperse
To faraway shores.
What spectacle greets your eyes?
Bloody cadavers in frightful heaps;
Scattered ruins; sanctuaries burned;
And mortals once happy,
Whom today misery has overpowered.
Good God! And why all this horror
That suddenly arms an uncouth mob
With steel and the power to kill?
Why? For an imaginary benefit
Of which they prait, for promises of bliss,

41

When their design is only to mislead the populace;
For the empty project, so often aborted,
Of establishing upon the earth
A Perfect Society, a Heaven
Which no people are yet capable
Of enduring or possessing.
Imbeciles! For a word you slaughter
Your brothers, your compatriots,
And even those friends, the foreign helots
Whom you feign to protect!

Those unfortunates! What were their conditions in their own barbaric countries from which they came? The picture made by all the voyagers is frightful. Transported to us, they became happier than the peasants of any nation; and not one regretted leaving his savage country. In self-concern alone, if not in humanity, was it not sufficient incentive for the colonists to take good care of his workers that they cost him much, that they rendered so much profit when they were healthy, and that they became so expensive when they were ill.

Those whippings of which one hears were always applied by one of their own comrades who had the talent of making more noise than pain, and only for faults which were punished much more severely elsewhere. This method of chastisement was adopted because the African, barely civilized, is considered a child and must be treated as such. He came from under the whip less marked, less humiliated, and less punished than our comrade D. ever was that certain day when, despite his eighteen years, our professor had him so nicely thrown out by the school porter. It is also that the skin of D., like that of any other European, is made from a different piece of cloth from that of which it pleased Nature to fabricate the hindquarters of the Africans, and it is this fact that these Philosophers have not realized.

" But these poor Negroes," they say, " work from morn till night." For my own part, I have never known a country where those that haven't a farthing to their names are not obliged to work from morn to night, and often from night to morn. The majority of human beings are unfortunately compelled to earn a living by the sweat of their brows.

> Fortunate, then, are those whom Fate has thrown
> Among the ranks of mortals condemned to work;
> And regulated by the grace of a wise economy,
> To work acording to their strength and capacity;
> Who, three times a day, in a comfortable place
> Are reunited to their families around an abundant table;
> Who, when the sun surrenders to the quiet night,
> These tired ones can, until the morrow,
> Be free from care and have their needed rest,
> Which love alone has the right to disturb;
> Who, when perchance misfortune does arrive,
> Do not die without help upon a bed of misery,
> But have the kind care of the healer's art
> About the couch where suffering reigns;
> And when age weighs upon their whitened heads
> Reducing them from strength to weakness,
> Who can, in the bosom of peace, await the moment
> That Heaven has marked for their lives to end.

Such was the existence of the Negro in the Colony of Saint Domingue. The laws made for their safety were very severe. No doubt with us, as elsewhere, some individuals infringed the laws; but all the French are not villains because France produces types such as Partouchen, Mandrin, Desrus, etc.; so, like these great criminals, the bad colonists were not always punished, the reason being a simple one: which is that in these islands, as upon the continent, or in America, Riches unfortunately has often the craft to throw a golden blindfold over the eyes of Justice. Besides, it is seldom that a colonist of Saint Domingue can be shown culpable of these pretended crimes that are believed to be common among us, and when they were committed, it was always done by a European, a Philosopher upon arrival, but a cruel Master two months later! The Creole makes a point of honor of being gentle and indulgent.

But if our slaves were so well treated, why did they revolt? One must ask those composers of phrases who have inundated our country with their incendiary writings; those stupid innovators who brought turmoil to France and killed their King; those Whites of Europe who were found at the head of the insurgents; those idiots who thought that the destruction of commerce would usher in a counter-revolution and who needed an army to sustain their new rights. One must take into account the jealousy, the Machiavellism of a rival nation, etc. One must find the reason, at last, in the character of all the ignorant populace, principally in the Negroes, like machines which can easier be made to start than to stop! These are the causes which started, accelerated, and prolonged the revolt, and destroyed the most beautiful country upon the earth.

I will have an infinite quantity of interesting details to give you upon this country which I should love, since she gave me birth.

> But today my hand, too weary,
> Refuses to aid my spirit,
> And never have I so much written;
> For this miracle, I give thanks

44

To Friendship, which alone knows
How to divest me of my sloth
Whose indolent subject am I.
Alas! May another Divinity
Unknown to me at present,
Terminate soon my misery,
Take me far from fields of War
And return me to where you are!

Book Two

᪥

ARGUMENT OF BOOK TWO

The author learns that his sister was offended that he did not address to her the first Book of his Odyssey, and decides to dedicate to her the second one. Entirely recovered from the wound which sent me back to the city, I leave with my brother-in-law for a camp which he is to command. That which transpires on the route. Trouble in the camp before our arrival and the dramatic action which the Commander took in re-establishing order. Recounting of two extraordinary repasts. The new Armida. Conflagration of all my estate. The attack and capture of a post. My single combat with a Mondongue; a rich prize. An amusing duel. A critical situation and my manner of getting out of it. I make a big discovery which brings me much glory and indigestion.

Camp Martelière, Saint Domingue

[MAY 1793]

MY very exacting sister thought ill of me for not having addressed to her the scribbling which I christened with the name: " First Book of My Odyssey." So I will try to reconciliate myself with her. The place I go to today does not offer, ordinarily, very amusing adventures; they are, however, the sort of ones I need, since this dear lady always loved more to laugh than to cry. Things must, after all, be taken as they come.

Each day, each week, each month, whenever I have the time or occasion, I shall write in my portfolio that which I have seen or found to be most striking. If the heavens carry me back safe and sound, then, with more leisure, I will sew together these transient fragments; I will intermingle them here and there with a madrigal like Demoustier's; then, with a humble air, I will present myself at the dressing-table of Madame, my manuscript in hand, and say to her: " Deign to receive the Second Book of my *Odyssey*."

They have come to inform me that my horse is saddled, my arms loaded, my servants armed. We leave for glory, or for anything which pleases hazard to have us encounter.

It was four o'clock in the morning; the sky was still azure; the air was soft and fresh; near the horizon, the brilliant clouds, resting close to the sea, announced the approach of the father of light. I called to your husband that Phoebus was leaving the arms of Thetis, and it was time for him, wretched mortal, to tear himself from yours.

49

He responded (and I do not know if it was after he had consulted you) that he was more like Hercules than Apollo; and that, besides, it had been centuries since the Sun-God had married, whereas he was still on his "honeymoon," as the English say; but that, nevertheless, after making his farewells (which I found a little long), he would join me. And then we departed.

In any other circumstances, we would, no doubt, go at a slow trot, making the long fatiguing route attractive by holding a pleasant conversation; but we were so full of sadness that it was impossible to speak; and our sole recourse was to run full speed at the risk of breaking our necks. As Boileau said: " Sadness jumps into the saddle and gallops with the knight who possessed her before departure." I said that shaking Sadness hard enough would cause her to lose her stirrup. This, at least, is what happened in our case. After an hour, speech returned to us, to the great contentment of our heroes, who profited by this to catch their breath.

I said to my companion: " My dear friend, how much I regret being obliged to leave the pleasures of the city. Ah! How one complains at separating oneself from objects one loves, to go to be enslaved in a dull camp, where one would die soon of boredom if one had not now and then the little pastime of a battle." Your faithful husband prefaced his response by an enormous sigh; then, getting to the subject, " And what would you say if you had to leave an adored wife? " And I replied " What about my Sophie—eh? It is a thousand times more difficult to abandon a mistress than a wife. Dear favorite one! Charming Sophie! "

And then we took to galloping for a half-hour, without opening our mouths. He is very agreeable, is your husband. Twenty-five, well built, handsome, intelligent, well informed, valorous in all tests—sometimes to the point of temerity. Our trip proved this last, and as soon as we arrive back safely, I can disclose the secret to you.

Being named Commander of the post established in the section of Terrier Rouge, my imprudent brother-in-law was not satisfied with the normal difficulties. He wanted to cross twenty-one miles of country infested with brigands, and where, until then, only armies dared pass. You know my sheep-like character; I go where I am called, and when your husband proposed that we go, " Just as you please," I responded. We mounted excellent horses, were armed like Amadis, and were followed by our brave and faithful equerries.

In crossing the erstwhile beautiful properties near Marin and Limonade, I experienced a sensation which I cannot describe. To be able to conceive it, one must be traveling, on an exquisite summer morning, over a country favored by Nature, and only encounter ruins, solitude, and scattered bones.

We were more fortunate than wise; no mishaps occurred. One time only, a group of Negroes seemed to dispute our passage. " Forward," cried your husband, in that terrible voice which you know, or rather, which you do not know; for it is not with that one, I presume, that he sighs to you of love, and being just married, he has not had occasion to refrain from using it before you. Upon the deafening " Forward! " we descended upon the amazed troups, who, perhaps, imagined that we were scouts from a large company, and so took to their heels, after saluting us with a volley of bullets, which had no other effect than to cover us with leaves.

We found in the camp only mounted militia. The new

Commander wrote to the general to make him realize the necessity to join the infantry and the artillery, which was a difficult thing to do. The officers of the regular troops thought themselves too important to serve under those whom they called " the Bourgeois." To satisfy all concerned, they took from various regiments sent from France, squads commanded by corporals; and all were put under the orders of a sergeant, whom they also sent.

This assistance we thought would prove fatal. Dissension arose between the newcomers and our militia. The sergeant, whose enormous moustache caused him to be called Carabi,* wanted to knife the Captain. He tried to encourage disorder, instead of looking for means to restrain it; and this would have been easy for him, since he was liked and feared by his comrades. He was a brave and good soldier, who had become spoiled by frequenting clubs, as had many others. He was in need of a good lesson to put him in his place. My brother-in-law took charge of doing that for him. He took a rather original manner of doing so, but at least it succeeded perfectly.

One morning, all the troups were under arms for the parade. We awaited the Commander and already Carabi was permitting himself the pleasure of passing some remarks about his chief's being a little late. He soon appeared, passed before the line slowly with a quiet but severe air. Arriving in front of the terrible Carabi, he stopped, measured him frigidly from head to foot, then addressed them all: " Soldiers, disorder is in the camp. The troops in the ranks are brave, doubtless, since they are French, but, until now, they have had no occasion to make us admire their courage, save to dare give forth

* Carabi was the name of a humorous character in an operetta of the time.

sarcasms against the intrepid Creoles whose exploits have proved their valor. They forget that the first duty of military training is subordination; they forget that if I did ask for them from the General, that it was less for them to help me in combat, than to give the militia the example of discipline."

The petty-officers, unworthy of the rank that was bestowed upon them, were the first to encourage these mutterings. Here, Carabi wished to speak. " Silence!" cried his chief, advancing upon him with a menacing manner. Then, resuming his discourse: " They think themselves humiliated to be under my command; ' A Bourgeois,' they say, ' a young dandy is not made to march at the head of old soldiers of the ranks.' Soldiers, I could make you submit, and I could punish you; I have the power and the means. But I prefer to prove to you that I am worthy to be your commander.

" Carabi, they praise your courage, your dexterity; your comrades obey you without scruple because they believe you to be their superior. Very well, step out of ranks if you dare. I will cease to be your chief; I prefer, for a moment, to abase myself to become your rival, and before the entire army, I challenge you to the arms you so favor." In pronouncing these last words, your husband drew his saber, and as Carabi seemed to hesitate: " Draw," he cried to him, " or I will cut you in half!" An order that had to be obeyed. This singular combat greatly astonished everyone; and poor Carabi, surprised, undecided, worried, rediscovered in his heart fine old sentiments, and stepping back, threw his saber at the feet of his adversary and said in an agitated voice: " Yes, you are my chief; yes, you are worthy of so being. How you can manage a two-edged sword! Let us make peace, my Commander. In the future I will prove to you that Carabi is a real French soldier; and may I lose my moustaches if you have ever to complain of me!"

This theatrical bit returned harmony to our little army. The soldiers have the greatest veneration for a chief who dared brave the redoubtable Carabi. As for the latter, his conduct at present is exemplary, and he has been most useful in all the details of the service which he knows perfectly.

When one fights, and when night and day one covers hills and dales, one must without doubt become very hungry. But to have an appetite is not all that is needed; one must procure the means of satisfying it; and this was one night we did not neglect doing so.

As we all here are a little epicurean, our delicate palates do not accommodate easily to our rations. Also, one of the first orders given to our patrol is to lay their hands on all the pigs and chickens of the country. Each night, when duties are assigned to the orderlies for the next day, three persons are named for hunting, and as many for fishing. As there is no good meal without dessert, we worked together to obtain it from the houses of the neighborhood.

We occasionally find ourselves reduced to our salted provisions, which we are obliged, by means of art, to suit to our tastes as much as possible. One day noon sounded, and all that was found in the stewards' quarters was dried cod-fish. What a prospect! The gastronomic counsel assembled. They proposed, they discussed; at last it was decided by voice vote that, for a week, we would give the nicest part of the dinner to the clever artist who would prepare, for that day, the tastiest plate of codfish. At once, those who believed in their genius began putting their hands to work.

Oh, what a fine art is that of cooking! We had for dinner eighteen plates of codfish, and not one resembled the others. It was a Provençal who captured the prize; and putting aside all artistic rivalry—for I also competed— I freely admitted that he merited the honor. It made you lick your fingers. Imagine a mixture of fish, oil, garlic, spices; and by a happy innovation of genius, which brought fine results, he introduced truffles, which until then did not seem to mix well save with fricassee of chicken.

For myself, yet a novice, I presented modestly a codfish *au gratin*. They thought the idea new and ingenious. I received second prize with a promise of the first leg of the turkey. But I well believe I got much favor by being the brother-in-law of the commander; for, between us, my fish was too peppery and my cheese smelled of smoke. In spite of anything that is said or done, protection will always prevail over merit.

Times of scarcity often follow times of abundance. For example, on your husband's birthday, we had a splendid repast. It consisted only of a single course, but certainly it was worth four. See if your mouth does not water: At the exact hour there appeared four mess boys in full-dress. They carried a litter upon which was placed a trough, on which was a whole veal, well roasted, and gently settled on a highly seasoned salad. The aforesaid calf was split from head to tail, and this opening was elegantly tied with pink ribbons. The trough was placed before the carver of that day, who untied the ribbons. The veal was separated enough to let be seen in his flanks a sheep prepared in the same manner, but tied with blue ribbons. In the mutton was an enormous turkey with

55

green ribbons. In this turkey was a capon tied with yellow ribbons; and the capon contained as many ortolans as there were guests. Imagine our further admiration and enthusiasm when, upon opening the little birds, which were encircled with strips of bacon rind, we found favors of different colors, each containing a marinated oyster! It was absolutely like the story, " In Rome there is a house, in the house there is a room, etc."

Toward the end of the meal, a delegation from the troops requested to present their respects to the Commander. They were told to enter. Carabi, like Coryphée, advanced, made three bows, coughed, and as he presented a large bouquet, sang an air of Grétry's: " It is for you that I arrange these flowers." When he got to the words: " Dear love, receive from Babet," he tried to give his voice a light graceful tone, which was in such ridiculous contrast to his gigantic form and enormous moustache, that we could not control a burst of laughter. Our gaiety did not at all disconcert our Mlle. Babet Carabi, who continued with his song in a serious, imperturbable manner.

In recognition of the compliment, we ceded our places to the delegation; and these gentlemen fell, as if famished, upon the remains of our dinner, devouring all, even to the pink ribbon.

One day, our fishermen, upon their return from the seashore, told us that a ship from Cap Français was grounded on a sand-bank near Caracol, and that a young and pretty passenger was found safe and sound in the wreck, but was desolately stranded on the shore. " Harness a carriage," said our gallant chief, " and the twelve handsomest young men of the camp follow on horseback."

If this order was given in good spirit, it did not prove so in judgment, as at the words " handsome young men," each one imagined that he was included, and the whole army was ready to leave. We then saw the necessity of making a choice, and to prevent civil war, it was ordered that only the most gallant should go. There were still murmurings, but nothing more followed; youth today prides himself less on gallantry than on looks.

The detachment started with the commission to find the beautiful one and to escort her to headquarters, with all the deference that should be shown the fair sex in misfortune. For a whole hour everyone had his eyes fixed on the road. As in Bluebeard: " My sister Anne, do you not see something coming? " At last sister Anne announced seeing clouds of dust. All were well attired and ready; the camp drums beat, the escort arrived, the carriage stopped, and our chief offered his hand to the interesting stranger. Presto! Our fisherman had reported well. Young, beautiful, and pleasant; she was all that. She was . . . guess if you can! You give up? Well, she was no more nor less than our neighbor on the Rue St. Marc, that elegant and voluptous Parisienne, without doubt the most beautiful woman in our country, that other Venus who not long ago took a new Vulcan as husband (it seemed appropriate that Mars should enter into her adventures). What, you yet do not know who she is? Then the I's must be dotted. Do you remember that devout old lady who lived near us? " Yes, you will say; " what a fresh, young face she has for a Venus! " Have patience! You have heard talk of the scene she had with our mother that day, when, with a confidential air, she reproached her for allowing you to associate with bad company. Mother was offended and insisted upon an explanation. The pious one claimed to have seen you from her window, laughing with this same voluptuous neighbor.

Mother proved to her that it could not have been. During the conversation, I was seated in a corner with downcast eyes and embarrassed mien; and mother began wondering if I could solve the enigma. She still remembered, one time in Paris, that she herself mistook me for you when I put on your dress. Being questioned, I was obliged to admit that it was I who had scandalized the eyes of the sainted lady. Meaning no harm, and only to pass the time, I had thought it amusing to change my trousers for your skirts. At this remark she called me to her side and gave a pathetic little sermon taken from St. Paul or St. Augustine, I do not know exactly from which.

She cautioned me particularly to protect myself from the skirts of this neighbor, as I would the Devil; and when I assured her that this beauty had affected me as did the robe of Dejauire,* she told me she did not remember having seen the name of that saint on the calendar, and asked me if she was a virgin or a martyr; to which I responded that she was a virgin, there was no doubt; but that it was not known precisely until what period; however, I added, she had a friend who had accomplished miracles. As she begged me to continue, I was about to recount to her the most celebrated and difficult deeds of Hercules, when my mother silenced me, and all was over.

My very dear sister, it was this same person of the forbidden skirts, according to our devout one, whom we had the honor and pleasure to possess in our camp. And thanks to several pretentions, we succeeded in keeping her for a day and night. You can well guess that we employed all the resources of our imagination to make

* An actress of that era noted for her scant apparel.

her visit as agreeable as possible; and like the Judge Daudin, who wished to amuse Isabelle with an entertaining spectacle, we proposed a pretty little battle, but we found she had no taste for such pastime.

The next day, the beauty in our midst could have furnished Tasso a song for his *Jerusalem*. It was indeed the enchantress Armida with the chaste Godfrey, and the crowd of young heroes, who offered all their services to Beauty in distress. Nothing was missing, not even the tender and impetuous Eustache, the young brother of the general. There was a detachment made ready to conduct our Armida to her home. All wanted to be included; save the wise Godfrey, who preferred trusting her to fate. What joys for those whom hazard favors; what despair for those whom it favors not!

At daybreak, Armida was put on her way, surrounded by her happy escorts in whom she soon included all those who had not been able to resist her charms. She arrived without accident, and instead of having us thrown in an obscure prison, as did the crafty daughter of Hidract, she gathered us in her salon with all care and hospitality, and would not let us leave before regaling us with a splendid and fastidious repast.

My sister, it is done; our ruin is consummated; I saw the turbulent flames, which were carried by the breeze in its course; I gazed upon the debris; I walked over the ashes still hot and red! What a day for me! What days, perhaps, with still worse to follow! Yesterday I was sitting tranquilly in my tent occupied in cleaning my firearms, when all of a sudden, toward the west of the camp, I saw a glow telling of an immense, encompassing fire. It was a spectacle the like of which we had often witnessed, and as usual, everyone tried to guess which place had become the new victim of conflagration. One who knew the localities perfectly cried out, "It is the P. plantation!" These words were as a thunder-clap to my ears. In the wink of an eye, I was on my horse, and at the head of about twenty dragoons; I cleared in an hour the long distance which separated the camp from our plantation. Alas! That hour was enough to annihilate the work of long years. The cowardly monsters! They fled at our approach; I could not immolate one upon the smoking remains of my fortune.

How you would have suffered if you could have seen the actual state of this place which, before our arrival, so much care was taken to develop: the sugar refinery, the vats, the furnaces, the vast warehouses, the convenient hospital, the water-mill which was so expensive, all is no more than a specter of walls blackened and crumbled, surrounded by enormous heaps of coals and broken tiles. The cruel ones had not even respected the houses of their brothers; and those homes for the Negroes, solid, safe, shaded by trees, enclosed by gardens, suffered the same fate as the home of the master. All the materials assembled at great expense for the construction of the beautiful new house we were going to build, were scattered or broken; and they did their work with great thoroughness. They demolished the aqueduct which conducted the river water to the great wheel of the mill; and they drained the pond by numerous irrigation trenches, that picturesque lake which carried such coolness to the habitation, and which always furnished such delicious fish. Why such fury in the devastation? Why deprive themselves of that which might have been so useful to them one day? It could not be out of hatred for us personally—we were complete strangers. We had been in France from our earliest years, and then the revolt broke out the day after our return, and so we were never allowed to live among them.

Here we are, my poor sister, completely reduced to misery. Before this last disaster, we had certainly lost much. When our sugar-cane, the source of our revenue, was burned, those laborers who remained faithful to us, who were brought together on the Jaquezi plantation, became more of an expense than a profit. But, at least, we had the hope of better times. Some days of work would have been sufficient to make repairs. But today, what a difference! Where can we lay hold of the enormous sums needed to reconstruct that crowd of buildings that resembled a little city?

Since my fate destines me to poverty, would to Heaven that I had been taken first. I would rather have lost the favors of Fortune before knowing of their charms. If I had been ruined in infancy, I would, no doubt, have been taught an occupation. I would certainly have become accustomed to the tastes and habits suitable to my new situation. O my sister! Reared as we were, I can only see ahead for us misery, privations, and sorrows. May the heavens inspire us, at any rate, with courage and strength to support them.

On my last page I was a little sombre; I had good cause. But at my age sorrows are not very lasting—one becomes consoled for everything, even misery. I have almost recovered my accustomed gaiety. By keeping active I dissipate sad thoughts which sometimes steal into my head. I join in all the detachments which each day scour the countryside. On Monday we attacked a Negro camp, where, for the first time, I saw bows and arrows used; the latter fell about us like rain, and the fear that they could be poisoned did not cheer us. Tuesday, during the night, we surprised in the midst of a thick forest a brigand chief who had established a seraglio. We seized his Excellency in the arms of a Senegalese Venus, who wanted, with all her might to tear our eyes out. She was furious— and with reason, the poor girl having hardly gotten in bed. Wednesday, we went to the *guildive,** where rum is made for the revolters. Each of us had blackened his face and hands in order to be able to pass for one of them; and Jean Pierre, my servant, presented himself as our commander. The conversation turned upon our camp. "Ah!" said the Negro chief, " if I could lay hold of the monkey who is their general, I would like to tear out his heart, cut it up like an onion, fry it, and have it for my breakfast." And that Monkey was simply your husband, who was with us—" Knave," cried he, in anger, " I am he!" Never have I seen a figure dissolve all at once as did this amateur hero, like a pillar of salt. He wanted to flee, but we seized him and his troop, and destroyed all their rum.

The most useful of our expeditions was that one which we made upon the plantation where they had assembled the cattle destined for Jean-François' army. We arrived there at the break of day; we were welcomed by two small volleys, which wounded three men and killed one. We fell with such rapidity upon the enemy that they had no time to re-load their guns.

Here we were in the camp, running from right to left as if we were running after something worth while. " Courage, my friends," we told our soldiers, " concern yourselves with gathering up harvests of braised meat and fricasseed veal. It is perhaps not as glorious as laurels, but more substantial." This harangue was a great

* A rum distillery.

success; each one did marvels. Your husband had the glory of taking prisoner General Jacquot, which is not a noble name, and will not shine in an epic poem, but that cannot be helped, and is not the fault of the conqueror.

As for me, my part was not as glorious. I had single combat with a large Mondongue Negro. We sparred for some time without wounding ourselves; he was stronger, I was more agile. At last he jumped for the little bottle of rum which I carry slung over my shoulder; happily, by a thrust well placed, I gave him a second mouth, a little beneath the one made by Nature; but I assure you that this time Art surpassed Nature by at least two inches.

The poor devil first gave a horrible cry, accompanied with a terrible grimace; then, drawing a pistol which he had hidden in his jacket, he aimed and fired. The ball lodged in my horse's shoulder. I was furious, and would have preferred myself to have been wounded, as the army doctor could cure me free of charge; whereas, if I lose my horse, I would not know where to get money to buy another.

While I was trying to dismount, my horse, which, let me say parenthetically, was frisking about like the best jumpers at Ashley, my adversary was trying to save himself by running through a hedge of lemon trees. His head and shoulders got by, but his hindquarters, which were enormous, could not follow. While he was in this position, hardly in decent costume, one of our militiamen, who by chance was passing by at that moment, ran his bayonet through his body. Astonished by this stroke, I got some information upon the one who made it, and was told he was the eldest son of a celebrated apothecary of Cap Français, which I doubted.

I realize the recitation of this combat is not worth

those of Patroclus and Hector, or a multitude of others, but each fights in his own way and recounts it as he can. After achieving the rout of the enemy, we occupied ourselves with the prize of victory. It was indeed no Golden Fleece, which gave such honor to the Argonauts. The remembrance of it makes me shudder.

Provided with booty, fruits of our valor, we made our way back to our camp. How we were received! The vaunted triumphs which honored the heroes of Rome after their victories were child's play compared to our brilliant entrance.

In the lead there marched with slow and majestic step, thirty beeves, fattened over a long time in sweet contentment. After them came about thirty cows, with large, well-filled udders, which made us anticipate cafe-au-lait and cream cheese. A dozen calves followed. They were at that happy age when skillful cooks recommend hanging them up after taking out the best part of their heads. The superb oxen, fastened with a yoke, seemed to look with self-satisfaction upon the hopes of their illustrious race. A number of innocent sheep, large and bushy, which we judged were descended from the herds of the Emperor of Morocco, advanced and playfully browsed on the grass of the plains. At last the march ended with six enormous sows worthy of the butchers of Mayence, and which were surrounded by an entire population of sucklings of both sexes and various weights.

For several days we have been completely idle. Around the camp, in about a seven mile radius, the country has enjoyed much rest, and our enemies, weary of their vain efforts, have retired into the inaccessible mountains, where it would be imprudent to search for them. We have had to pass the time doing something. Each one proposed different amusements; and I will recount to you those with which we gaily occupied ourselves during the last week.

We have among us a young man whom Nature seemed to have made expressly to be the butt for jokes. He recently arrived from a French province, and for the first time found himself separated from his paternal roof. Some unkind jesters, after having taken his measure, resolved to amuse themselves. To begin with, they made him believe that the Governor wished to recompense the valor which he showed in the last affair by elevating him to a captaincy. They requested him to accept the uniform of his new rank. He received, by special courier, the letter from the Governor, the commission, and the uniform. Our man was delighted, and he was easily persuaded to get dressed up right away in the honorable uniform. This was of heavy material, doubled and loaded with at least ten pounds of braid, as well as epaulets. Note that this uniform, although of extraordinary length, was extremely tight. Also, judge the punishment the unfortunate one took by insisting upon wearing it; he who could but poorly accustom himself to our burning climate and melted under a simple cotton jacket. It was at the table, particularly, that he suffered most. They allotted him the duty of carving the roasts, and hampered as he was, it was truly an extraordinary problem. This pleasantry, too long carried on, became a cruelty. They dropped it after two days, only to replace it with another.

A supposed friend confided to our new captain that he was being mocked, and proved to him that he could not let pass such an insult without demanding satisfaction of the one who had invented the idea. The captain accepted the confidence well enough, since the pleasure of being

65

able to take off his exhausting uniform consoled him for the pain of losing his glorious rank. Exactly what was signified by " demanding satisfaction " was explained to him, and he declared that his godfather, a churchwarden, had always told him that it was a grave sin, so that he could, in conscience, only fight with his fists. " And I am ready," he said, while brandishing fiercely his two arms, " to make him see stars!" They succeeded, however, in having him follow the usual procedure, causing him to send a challenge to La —, who had offered himself to be the scapegoat.

Towards evening, the belligerent parties were escorted by a half-dozen official witnesses; about a hundred others, hidden in the underwood, came upon the battlefield about a mile from camp. It was decided, for a good reason, that the combat was to be with pistols. At a signal each would fire. La — gave out a wounded cry, which all repeated in echo, and he made three turns à la Vestris, two somersaults, one quiver, and lay down upon the ground, taking pains to unbutton his vest to allow his shirt to be seen all covered with India fig stain as blood. " Oh, my God, my God," cried the anxious victor, bewildered and beside himself! " You can see I must have killed him! What have I done, and what will my godfather say? Sirs, I swear to you I did not do it on purpose." " No lamentations are necessary," replied the witnesses; " he is not dead yet and he must be taken to camp to have his wound dressed. It is your affair, Sir, and we will place him upon your shoulders."

" Ah, willingly, my friends. Poor La —, how he is suffering! Do you think he will survive? And this was the first time I have ever fought a duel. Oh! what will my godfather say? "

Bending beneath his load, sweating large drops, the godson of the godfather staggered back to camp, diverting his escorts with all kinds of lamentations. At each step, his victim moved and held tighter around his slayer's neck, or kicked him in the shins, and the poor devil took all that for the last agonies of the dying.

On arriving at the hospital the scene became more pathetic. The wounded one was laid upon a stretcher. The surgeon arrived with a basket filled with saws, knives, needles, scissors, and bandages. He gravely rolled up his sleeves; he probed the wound, reflected, examined, considered; then, approaching the desolated victor: " Bloodthirsty one," he said, " what have you done? If only you had aimed a foot more to the right, it would be only a trifle. The unfortunate victim of your vengeance would have missed having his pancreas separated from the tonsils of his scrotum, but, by the course of the deadly ball, one sees very well that you aimed intentionally at the cerebral thatch of the femur. Yes, gentlemen, it is only too true. Approach and see for yourselves. O, memorable wound! The celebrated sons of Aesculapius never saw a similar one on the bloody fields of Pergamos. See, look, all of you. Here, I find the left spleen pushed against the occipital tibia ; there, the hard core of the clavicle crowding hard the abdomen of the mastoid gland and emptying all the gastric juices into the Fallopian tubes. And what is more, gentlemen, that which will astonish most the men of our art, is that no trace can be found of the mesentery in the jugular of the xiphoid bone, and that is why the wound is fatal."

At this word, the only one he understood in this anatomy lecture, the poor devil cried out disconsolately, " Fatal! O, my God, my God, what will my godfather say? Doctor,

I swear that I did not see either the cerebral thatch or the femur of the mesentery, since I never knew where they were situated. And, besides, I do not see well. Fatal! Fatal! Ah! What will my godfather say?" And the unfortunate ran from one to another swearing that he never did it intentionally.

To vary the scene, the injured one desired to make his will. He was brought paper and ink. One witness wrote the dictated last wishes. At each bequest his assassin responded with a long sigh to which he added, while raising his eyes: "Ah, what a kind heart!" The last bequest, however, was attended with tears. "La, he leaves me a plantation of vermicelli and of macaroni upon the mountains of Gonave, and all to prove that he holds no rancor." The inheritor of such good fortune could not help but cry aloud, "Oh! If he only had consented to hold a fist fight, he would not have finished with contusions; I would give all the vermicelli that grows on the isle to recall him to life."

However, as we were signaled that supper was ready, it was necessary to think of clearing up the plot of the comedy. The dying one, who was only dying of hunger, asked to be carried in. He asked to embrace his adversary as a sign of reconciliation. The adversary approached in haste and had already opened his arms when, all of a sudden, the agonized one jumped upon his neck and made faces and screamed as if insane. Our captain, frightened, struggled and disengaged himself, and ran as if the Devil was chasing him. One of the witnesses followed, stopped him, and said with a serious air, " Sir, you have often confessed a desire to be received as a Freemason. The principal virtues required by that order are courage and sensitiveness. It was essential to be sure that you possessed these, and the events of today were a test. You have acquitted yourself with honor; so, Sir, tomorrow you will be admitted into the respectable temple of Solomon. Your antagonist, who is as willing as you or I, will serve you at the table to repay you with a good supper for the fatigue of a night, which, far from meriting the reproaches of your godfather, the churchwarden, will cover you with glory in his eyes as in those of posterity." One could only imagine the cheerful look that came to our hero. " Oh, I am so relieved that he will not die," he cried, jumping for joy. Then he added, " Indeed, I am almost spent. If the ball had gone a jot farther, I would have killed him surely." The next day he was received as a member of the association to which he so much wanted to belong; he only lacked a small formality on his diploma: it was that of all who signed it, not one had the honor of being a Freemason.

I was on a mission to the camp of General Pajot, a brave Creole and friend of my brother-in-law. One morning we were discussing the deplorable news which had just been brought us. The Mulattoes of the East, who long since joined the insurgents, claimed to repent of this action, and requested to reunite themselves with the Whites, and they were accepted in the town of Ouanaminte. They at first showed great fidelity, but when by dint of guile they had dulled the vigilance of the Whites, they fell upon the garrison, pitilessly cutting the throats of all the inhabitants they could capture, and returned with plunder to the party they feigned to abandon.

The knowledge of this horrible treachery was well calculated to worry us. Our soldiers were, in part, Men of Color, faithful up to now, but who would cease to be so. We were discussing this matter, when our guards

advanced and notified us that two Mulattoes, carrying a
flag of truce, asked to speak to the chief. They were told
to enter, and here is the subject of their mission. The celebrated Candi, that bloodthirsty Mulatto, whose greatest
pleasure would be to pull out the eyes of the Whites with
a corkscrew, made the offer to turn himself over, and
swore himself and two hundred of his followers to submission and good conduct.

The moment was well chosen; however, this merited
consideration. This brigand's large force, which was well
disciplined and completely armed, had cost us dear for the
victories we had won over them. They had harrassed
us without cease; they devastated the country; they encouraged desertion of our soldiers who belonged to their
own caste. If we accepted their offer, that would at least
make fewer of them to combat. But were they, perhaps,
only working some perfidy? In this case, we had learned
by what had happened to us in the East, and could we
not, with precautions, foil their scheme. Pajot, much
embarrassed, delayed his answer until a courier could
return whom he was sending to the Governor. The
Governor, more embarrassed than we, got out of the
affair by giving us full power—submitting, he said, to
our judgment.

After long consultations, Candi was told that, as a
security measure, we required that he send to our camp
all the families of his soldiers, after which he would
receive further orders. Three days later we saw arrive
a large group of women and children. Since they were
exhausted and covered with tatters, we concluded that it
was to misery and want that we owed the conversion of
their fathers and husbands. The group was put under
surveillance and Candi was ordered to descend to the

town of Trou, situated between his camp and ours, but abandoned since the Negro revolt.

When our yellow Excellency made known his arrival, Pajot went to him escorted only by twenty dragoons; I went along as his aide. We found the Mulattoes in battle formation. At each end of their rank was a cannon. A few feet ahead was Candi—the horrible Candi. What a face! What eyes! It seemed one could read in them the long list of victims whose throats he had cut! It seemed one could read the wild desire to butcher again and the regret at not being able to do it! The monster, dressed in a jacket of ticking, upon which showed the two epaulets of a General, with pistols in his belt and a saber at his side, advanced towards us, with a forced air of submission and respect. After a parley of half an hour, when all the terms of capitulation were fixed, Pajot lifted his voice, and in the Governor's name, received Candi as commander of the town. The bewildered Mulattoes were sent to establish a garrison. He proclaimed afterwards, in the customary way, the one who had been designated as second in command. Hardly had he named a big Mulatto, when a sinister figure stepped out of rank with a menacing attitude, and in an insulting voice, cried, " I have, up to now, been the lieutenant of Candi; I should still be, I want to be, and will be." At those words, we spontaneously placed our hands to our sabres. The Mulattoes carried arms, and Candi, with a worsted expression, cast his eyes savagely upon us, then upon his comrades. But Pajot, almost beside himself, with an infuriated look and raging voice, cried " Scoundrel." Then, sword in hand, he advanced on the culprit. This one, intimidated, retreated to the middle of the troops, who seemed disposed to defend him. " Put down your arms!" said Pajot in a terrible voice. After a minute of uncertainty, they obeyed but with murmurings. Then our intrepid chief advanced towards Candi and ordered him to have the insolent rebel arrested. Candi seemed to hesitate; Pajot advanced upon him, jerked from Candi's belt one of the pistols he had there, and ordered, " Arrest that man, or I will blow off your head." The Mulatto ground his teeth in rage; but recalling, no doubt, the powerful motives which made him offer to give himself up, he decided to do what had been demanded. He began with several excuses, then harangued his troops, exhorting them to submission, and after giving orders, four men seized and escorted the so-called lieutenant before our General. He would be shot. We all trembled. We thought he was going too far, that never would they execute such an order, and already we were preparing to sell our lives at a high price, since these brigands would surely try to kill us. To our great surprise, we saw them only making supplications to try to save their comrade.

" He deserves death," said Candi, " I know it, but I implore your leniency. He is a very good soldier; I have always been satisfied with his services. If I did not suggest him as my second it was only because he sometimes drinks, and today you can see for yourself, he is drunk and can hardly remain standing." Pajot remained inflexible.

" Is this," he asked, " the first proof you give me of your repentance? Is this the blind submission that you swore to me? Is this the recompense for the care I have given your suffering families? I received them when they were perishing in misery, and now they have in abundance everything they need—things which they have lacked for a long time, and as for yourself, right now

72

they are preparing, at my orders, to be as lavish with you." These artful allusions reminded the Mulattoes of their situation and of the hostages whom they had placed at our mercy.

All was being made ready for the fatal execution. Already the victim was upon his knees and the bandage was over his eyes. Eight bewildered soldiers were preparing their arms; they only awaited the signal. " I will pardon him," said Pajot, and a long cry of joy resounded in the air. " I will pardon him, but he must enter the ranks and learn how to obey before he thinks himself worthy to command. Mulattoes, I did not come to you. It was you, who, in full accord, beseeched me to receive you. If you regret this step, there is yet time; go and return to your dens. You know that if I learn the way there, I will again fight you and defeat you. But, if for reasons which I shall not go into, you decide to remain under my orders, I will demand that you respect my authority. I will punish you with rigor, as I will reward you with generosity."

The Mulattoes responded to this harangue by new oaths of good conduct; and after giving them orders as to their duties, we returned to the road towards our camp, all of us astonished at finding ourselves still alive.

You will realize that, whatever their promises, we did not wholly trust their intentions. They were entirely isolated from us; they received only enough to live on for a day at a time; and their munitions were sufficient only for their safety. They never made their way into our retrenchments; and their wives were allowed to see them a few at a time and in turn. In this way, I believe you can be free of anxiety, and that we will get out of this better than we did at the garrison at Ouanaminte.

I come from covering myself with glory; I come from rendering my name famous; this name, until now so little known, I hear repeated about me with enthusiasm! Listen, and join your admiration to the crowd who carry me on their shoulders.

The sun, which heavy clouds prevented for eight days from warming the earth, broke all at once the barriers which dared oppose its rays. It reappeared more resplendent than ever. The damp sod received with avidity its life-giving blaze; the trees again lifted their sleeping branches; and the fields, almost flooded, became resplendent with brightly bursting flowers.

To salute the tutelary divinity of our countryside, I emerged from my refuge of that dull camp where the noisy games harassed me; I went for adventure, and I freely joined forces with the singing birds, who, perched on the swaying branches, were drying their wings and warbling.

Entranced at the pleasure one finds in wandering in the country after a forced retreat of several days, I advanced to the side of the enemy, farther than prudence permitted. I was alone and almost unarmed. A noise in the foliage of a neighboring wood recalled to me the danger of my situation. I prepared to take the road back to camp, when, on the side of a hill, my eyes glimpsed for a moment the long expanse of a solitary valley where, doubtless, no mortal had penetrated in a great while. There I saw . . . O surprise! O enchantment! There, I tell you, I saw, at the edge of a brook, where the limpid waters murmured over golden sand, in all the burst of its freshness, surrounded with that inexpressible charm which Nature lavishes upon her masterpieces, I saw—a bed of immense mushrooms! Yes, Madame, mushrooms of the finest variety, white above and pink beneath; a novice could not mistake them. There were enough to stuff all the turkeys in the colony. Judge of my joy; not for a year had we eaten any, and all the amateurs of the camp, after useless research, were persuaded that none existed within a radius of fifteen miles.

I realized right away the importance of my discovery, and I hastened to return to the army in order to inform them. By the quickness of my footsteps, by the excitement of my looks, by, I know not what strangeness in my manner, they imagined I was bringing a piece of extraordinary news. They rushed to me, they surrounded me. It was in vain, as I only wished to speak in the presence of the general. And he, informed of what was happening, came up to me; then, mounting upon a rock in order to be seen by all, I said, " Gentlemen, and all of you who hear me; I have been over two miles from our encampment; I walked over the hills and dales that separate us from our savage enemies; when Fate, tired, no doubt, of persecuting us, discovered to me an inexhaustible mass of the most superb mushrooms. I can swear this upon my head; Beauvilliers, himself, taught me in the past to know them. Command, Sir, that all our orderlies of the army, defended by an invincible escort, go secure a treasure so necessary to the well-being of our warriors. As for myself, as my only recompense, I claim the honor to name the sauce to accompany the first platter on which it will be served at our table."

I was still speaking, when the dazzled crowd all about me accorded eulogies of praise and thanks.

O vanity of vanities! O vicissitudes of humanity! Of all the joys purchasable, Glory, the sweetest, often costs the most. Which no one can prove better than I. So

75

recently was I full of enthusiasm and rapture; well, these same mushrooms, the cause of my happiness, were also the cause of my suffering. In vain, having them cooked by all the rules of good home cooking; in vain, having them swimming in oil, spiced with pepper, surrounded with parsley and shallots—my weak stomach could not support their strange richness, and I write you, hardly recovered from the throes of a dreadful case of indigestion.

Book Three

⤠

ARGUMENT OF BOOK THREE

A long chain of unhappy events threw the author upon the North American continent. He recounts it to a young lady who had the goodness to be interested in his situation. Commissioners sent by France arrive on the Cape with a new general and several war ships. Dark intrigues of the two Commissioners to divide their duties. An earthquake. After three days and three nights of combat, having lost all hope, having seen slaughtered my best friends, thinking my family the victims of flames, without money, or clothing, consumed with fatigue, and my heart full of despair, I embarked on board the squadron of Admiral Sercé with those inhabitants who escaped from the conflagration and the dagger's point. I recover my family, hear recounted what occurred to them. A few details upon the new English speaking country. The adventure in the Inn. News of France. Love consoles me for my misfortune.

To A. M. L. R.

I would forget in the arms of Love
The misfortunes long and cruel,
Which lately have clouded my days,
And you wish that I recall for you
These despairing memories!
You wish, in these short moments
When I could, my faithful love,
Adorn your young features
With roses of joy,
That I surround you with cypress,
That sad emblem of suffering!
I obey! You shall now share
Those woes which I must retrace;
But when upon my heart you weep,
I will so grateful be
If my burning lips can efface
The tears which you will shed.

YOU were a witness to the first disaster of our unhappy colony; but your prudent family foresaw the melancholy future, and put themselves under the protection of the hospitable skies of the United States of America. There you learned, no doubt, how much pain we had to experience in order to save from the flames some portions of our country that were of personal interest; among others, was the opulent city of Cap Français. We succeeded only in retarding its fall; a cruel event finally destroyed it, and I will try to paint for you the deplorable circumstances. Perhaps you have been told of the first troubles, which were set off by the arrival of the civil Commissioners, P. and S. They came from France with the old Count d'E., who replaced M. de B. in the Government of Saint Domingue. To inspire the respect of the Whites and the fear of the Negroes, we received the new Governor with all the civil and military honors which he merited elsewhere, for his name, rank, and years.

> But all these pompous ceremonies
> Offended the modest eyes
> Of the new Commissioners.
> One knows that the Republicans
> (Men of very strong principles)
> Look always with disdain
> Upon fame and great honors
> Given to any but themselves.

Those whom France sent us, under the pretext of aiding and re-establishing order, had as their secret mission the destruction of everything. They could not look without rancor upon the soldier and the inhabitant rallying around the new chief, and swearing to sacrifice their opinions, quietude, and lives for the general good of the country. These men organized Jacobin Clubs, and by their intrigues, they succeeded at last in detaching from the government a portion of the national battalions, which had recently disembarked, and that crowd of artisans known as " little-whites." They surrounded themselves with the Mulattoes and commenced sowing among the slaves of Cap Français those seeds of revolt which have since borne fruit so horrible.

Soon our citizens, menaced, insulted,
Could not, without peril, leave their homes.
An emancipated mob, rabble of our cities,
Dared to look upon us with insolent eyes.
The slaves, heretofore dutiful and filled with zeal,
Commenced to show a rebellious heat.
Our lukewarm soldiers, prodded by traitors,
Already placed a price on their allegiance.
The people were encouraged in license,
While talents, virtues, and duties were expelled;
One saw only vice and ignorance arise,
And the city delivered to disorder and conspiracy;
In our fields new fires burned each day
And to the foot of the parapets was the plain devastated
By unpunished brigands who were no longer denounced.

Disorder was complete when the General, too late, tried to destroy the cause. He ordered the abolition of the Clubs. Then, the Commissioners finally raised their masks and declared themselves to be the sole masters. They notified the old and feeble d'E. that he should embark immediately, with all his officers of the regiment at the Cape.

At this impudent demand, the regular troops, the volunteers, and all the honest inhabitants gathered upon the field of battle and swore obedience and protection to the General. That was the moment to act, and if d'E. had possessed the least energy, we would still be in our country. But it pleased them to scheme, to deliberate, to harangue; they had scruples, made tempting reconciliations; and these delays chilled enthusiasm. On the other hand, the Commissioners were active—they had seized the Arsenal for themselves, and, provided with arms and ammunition, they marched at the head of a wild populace to the place where we were engaged in discussion. The two parties were only separated by twenty paces. The irritated chiefs ran from one side to the other, inciting their soldiers, decrying their antagonists; several more modest ones proposed compromises; some signaled for butchery; some for the delay of it. It was all terrible. Our side was more disciplined; that of the Commissioners, more numerous; there were, besides, six pieces of cannon pointed at us within range of pistol shot.

> O sad result of civil discords!
> Among these hostile cohorts
> I saw, near enough to pierce my breast,
> A furious fighter, who, before this unholy hour,
> Would have given for me his life and fortune.
> He had shared my morning repast;
> We left each other with a clasp of hands.
> Ah! that lately friendly hand was
> Ready to turn against me now a flaming faggot;
> That eye, whose sweet expression I had admired,
> Pierced me now with menacing rage.
> His first cannon fire
> Would reduce to bloody powder,
> Me, who only yesterday was his closest comrade!

While our chiefs were disputing, in the center of the opposing ranks, the secret emissaries were profiting by the tumult and disorder and suborning our soldiers. They succeeded only too well. Already several had deserted; others were muttering; one heard the word " aristocrats " come from several enemy mouths. At last, be it from humanity or from weakness, the old General announced he did not want more slaughter for his cause. *His* cause! It was our Cause and not his! The main thing was to prevent the colony from falling under the claws of two tigers who wanted to tear it to pieces. The two tigers triumphed and the old and timid sheep was sent, under guard, aboard one of the vessels of the squadron.

> Leaders of the people, show your energy and skill
> To do worthily in this twisted world
> Your numerous duties in the needed task!
> For you, the peaceful virtues are not enough.
> These virtues, that adorn the plain citizen,
> In the public man make disaster for the state.
> O you, whom all the universe knows for your beneficence,
> You, who are admired for your principles and sincerity,
> Good father, good husband, O Louis, O my King!
> Despite your virtues, you have cost France
> More blood than ever was lost by Rome
> Through vicious Nero or the cruel Sulla!

Our little army, deprived of its chief, dispersed. The victorious party spared the infantry, because they might have use of it, but the poor inhabitants were pursued in the streets, and many were massacred before they could find refuge. By a happy chance, I discovered one right away, with a man who was preparing to leave for another part of the island; and profiting by the night, I embarked with him. Hardly had our launch touched the shore where we were going, when someone came aboard in order to warn us that the municipality, having been " Jacobinized " by the Commissioners, would not receive any individual without a passport signed by their hands. My friend had one for himself and for a white domestic; and he proposed that I play the part.

The one in whose service I was enlisted received orders to remain on the launch until it sailed and to return to the Cape. Unfortunately for me, he became fatigued of his prison, and to distract himself, he went to drink a pint at the tavern on the pier! He was detained, questioned, recognized; and I, pursued again, only found safety in the woods of the wild mountains. After several weeks stay in this savage retreat, I learned, by chance, that the Commissioners, after having gotten everything at the Cape under their submission, had left for Port-au-Prince in order to repeat the self-same scenes. I thought I could, without danger, leave that solitude which was not at all in accord with my tastes; and I secretly got to the post that was commanded by my brother-in-law. I passed some time, occupied without respite in the laborious duties of war. A serious illness obliged me to seek rest and the care of my family at the Cape. I was scarcely convalescing before the two Commissioners reappeared in the Northern province, still soiled with the blood they had spread in the province of the West. One could foretell their design, one knew their character; everyone saw the storm forming, without doing anything to divert it; so true it is that one cannot escape one's destiny.

In order to mix, now and then, a gentler hue with the sombre color of my report, I may be permitted, while speaking of two monsters, to speak also of two lovers who never did harm to anyone by comparing the inaction of my fellow citizens to my own conduct when you came to me.

> When, into my rustic retreat,
> You came and transformed it,
> I foresaw my approaching defeat
> And did not try to prevent it.
> By one bitter experience
> I had learned to my cost
> That Love for each of its joys
> Exacts a thousand torments.
> But here with new rays of hope

Love appeared to my eyes again,
And I surrendered without defense
To the fresh wounds it would give me.

How much good fortune I owe to that happy heedless-
ness! How much ill fortune have not all of us experienced
from that other fatal defeat, since the arrival of those
scoundrels who spread desolation among us.

These Commissioners who were sent to Saint Domingue
were received with enthusiasm by the Negroes and the
Mulattoes. The women of these two castes escorted their
carriages, waving in the air branches of palms and crying,
" Long live our leaders and our avengers! " These men
with smiles on their lips and fury in their hearts caressed
them and promised them help and protection, in the name
of the French Republic and of Heaven. Of Heaven!
The hypocrites!

Outraged Heaven, no doubt, flung back
Their promises, their impious vows;
By a sad omen were we warned
To abandon this place dedicated to the Furies.
Three times, the sea roared with rage
And cast itself upon the land, half drowning it.
Beneath the staggering feet of a terrified throng
Three times the earth did tremble.
One would have said in those awful days
That the universe shuddered in advance
At the sad fate that threatened
A people once happy and peaceful.

I still recall with dread this terrible phenomenon. It
was in the middle of a scorching night; the air, heavy
and humid, was not stirred by a single breath; and yet
one could hear the efforts of the clouds in movement, and

the horizon had the color of blood. After having returned, worn out, to my bed a hundred times, an overpowering sleep closed my eyelids when all at once a loud and prolonged noise awakened me. I tried to guess the cause; it resembled nothing I had ever heard before. Soon after, the house shook, the furniture fell over, the walls split with an unheard of cracking sound. I bounded from my bed and rushed to the street. The debris from roofs was falling on all sides; masters and slaves ran in confusion here and there, emitting with difficulty from their fear-tightened throats the sinister cry: " Earthquake! "

I returned to the square nearest our city dwelling. There, I found all the inhabitants of my neighborhood. The men were in consternation; the women, half naked and hysterical, believed it to be the end of the world. The children and the servants joined their cries to the howling of the dogs and whinnying of the horses. Three tremors, a short distance from each other, redoubled the terror, the disorder, and the tumult; and no one dared re-enter his house for fear of being crushed beneath its crumbling walls. What a night of anguish! Day came, and all was forgotten. Everyone went back to his accustomed work, or to his favorite pleasure, not worrying whether or not the city was beside a volcano ready to erupt!

It was a new spectacle for me, this earthquake, and since I had come out of it safe and sound, I was not sorry to have witnessed it, in order to be able to speak of it with knowledge. We experienced a half dozen of them in the short space of time which preceded the burning of the city.

It soon arrived, that fatal moment which saw our last refuge reduced to cinders, spilled the blood of thousands of victims, and plunged an entire population into despair

BATTLE IN SAINT DOMINGUE

"We charged upon them, without hesitation in using our bayonets."

THE BURNING OF CAP FRANÇAIS

" They arrived with torches and knives and plunged into the city. From all sides flames were lifted as in a whirlwind and spread everywhere."

and misery. How can a hand so unpracticed as my own undertake to draw this event in all its horrible details?

> O for one who could guide my lyre
> To intone this anguish! To sing of your charms
> Love has encouraged and inspired me,
> But which deity will aid me to paint those crimes?
> Crimes! What a word to pronounce
> When my heart is full of you!
> For this sacrilegious mixture
> I ask pardon on my knees.
> If, in sketching the crimes of the Earth,
> I use at times the pencil stroke of Love,
> Do not reproach me this needed relief;
> For when sorrow casts me into despair,
> Your image is my only consolation.

A new Governor arrived from France to replace the Count d'E. But the Commissioners had become too well accustomed to the taste of supreme authority to consent to letting themselves be removed; they had too well succeeded once before in dislodging an importunate superior to fear undertaking to do it again. After a glance, they had measured their man. Without bothering about orders from France, they had the newcomer unceremoniously arrested and placed on board one of the waiting vessels. Those amongst whom the Governor found himself there became interested in his behalf, and the squadron presently laid itself broadside, bringing the city into the range of its cannon; and on Tuesday, the twenty-fourth of June, they vomited on our shores a hoard of undisciplined sailors, under the orders of a chief who was far from having the talents and energy which were demanded for such an enterprise.

Like two evils of which we must choose the lesser, the

youth of the Cape lined up on the General's side and the regular troops followed example. The Commissioners reunited under their flag the free men of color and the little-whites. They had no shame, and in consequence embraced in their ranks these same slaves in revolt which the Mother Country had ordered them to subdue. So Discord, with a dagger in one hand and a torch in the other, gave, at last, the signal for civil war.

Still weak from an illness which was hardly terminated, I was, besides, on that day, overburdened from the effects of a very strong medicine. However, I got up and took my weapons. My family tried in vain to dissuade me; deaf to their prayers, insensible to their tears, I tore myself from the arms of those who were most dear to me in this world and I went to join the brave volunteers, already fighting in the Montarché Square. We did not yet well know for whom, or against whom, we must fight. A column of Mulattoes soon ended our uncertainty. They had come secretly from the barracks, and when they believed they had us in range, they began giving us a rain of heavy musket fire; we charged upon them, without hesitation in using our bayonets. This troop was half destroyed and the rest, being afraid, took refuge in the Government Garden.

Alas! That combat was for me the cruelest of these disastrous days. We lost the young Chevalier de B., the kindest of men, and my most intimate friend. Hardly twenty-two years of age, he had already risen by merit alone to become a captain of artillery in the regiment of Metz. Conditions years before had caused his family, like ours, to come to Saint Domingue, where he was born; and like me, that day he joined the volunteers at the Cape. Inspired by his fiery courage, he followed the Mulattoes into the garden, where they were hiding. Cannon fire, shot from the peristyle, broke his leg. He fell at the moment when new troops came out of the arsenal and attacked us from the rear. In the momentary disorder, occasioned by this unexpected attack, the absence of the Chevalier de B. was not observed, and he remained at the mercy of the Mulattoes, who let him perish without help or consolation.

> My poor friend! Just the eve before
> Had we two, in a moment of leisure,
> Planned beneath a flowering tree
> Our future studies and delights.
> " Our close friendship began in our dawning years,"
> He said, smiling in tender memory.
> " May we never part and may
> That sacred knot, which honored our youth,
> Unite us ever until we die."
> Ah! if the fate which separated us
> Permits me to see once more my unhappy country,
> I swear by your shade, my dearest friend,
> To go in search amongst the debris,
> For the spot that holds your ashes.
> A tomb there will tell of my loss and of your sacrifice,
> And each day, there I will come
> To adorn it with greenery and water it with tears.

You cannot form an idea of the excesses, the wrongs, the crimes, of that deplorable day. I saw artillerymen, against every remonstrance, aim a thirty-six pound cannon against a single man, fire, miss their target, but blow up a house. I saw marines fire in the air, because they complained of not having enough powder. I saw musketmen always insisting on being preceded by militia-men. I saw a general, frightened by a false alarm, throw himself into the sea to rejoin his barque, crying, " Every man for himself." I saw dragoons proudly leading us and haranguing us into excitement, who, when they had accompanied us as far as the batteries of the enemy, turned upon us a murderous fire and retired amidst the ranks of our adversaries, laughing at our credulity.

After many consultations, it was decided to attack, in order, the quarters of the Commissioners. The army started off in three columns. The one in which I served, composed of Creoles, was sent into the mountains, and succeeded by force of arms in placing a cannon on an isolated hill which dominated the stronghold. This advantageous position helped us so much that, upon the twelfth discharge, we saw the enemy in disorder abandon their retreat and take the road to the plain. Emboldened by our success, we decided to pursue them. Our march was often interrupted by insurgent Negroes. We advanced despite their attacks and their numerous ambuscades, and, towards nightfall, we entered Cap Français.

Upon our entry into the city, we were stupefied with astonishment. The streets were deserted, the houses closed. No noise, no movement, nothing to announce the proximity of an army victorious or defeated. Arriving without difficulty at the arsenal, we found only those who had been stationed there to guard it; they informed us that the General, overcome by a panic which no event could explain, had re-embarked in haste, followed by the soldiers and sailors!

Left to ourselves, without a superior officer, without supplies, without ammunition, and overcome by fatigue and hunger, we decided to spend the night resting upon our guns, near the shore, leaving to the morrow the making of any decision. That night was, for us, a long and sad one.

The creeping hours were hardly half run out when, all at once, horrible shrieks resounded in our ears; a great brightness lit the black skies. From the summit of the mountains down the roads to the plain, came immense hoards of Africans. They arrived with torches and knives and plunged into the city. From all sides flames were lifted as in a whirlwind and spread everywhere. What a spectacle of cruelty! I can still hear the whistling of bullets, the explosions of powder, the crumbling of houses; I can still see my brave comrades contending vainly against steel and fire; I still see the feeble inhabitants in flight, half-naked, dragging in the streets, in the midst of accumulated debris, the mutilated corpses of their families or their friends. In such terrible moments danger to those dear to us makes us forget danger to ourselves. I joined a troop of determined young Creoles, and we went from house to house to snatch from death those whose weakness prevented them from trying to escape. Twenty times, with them, I tried to penetrate the line to my house, which was situated in the center of the enemy holdings; twenty times, repulsed by a superior force, we returned with despair in our souls, and succeeded only in bringing back the bleeding remains of some of our comrades.

Alas! Whilst with horror,
I cried at my powerless efforts;
All the cherished objects of my heart
Remained prey to this terror,
Without remedy, without hope!
I, lying upon the earth, spent, desolate,
Could see the hastening fire

Rising from their collapsing roof.
I accused myself of parricide;
I felt that I had been called
By my plaintive sisters, by my dying mother:
Hapless Ones! I was son and brother,
Yet, when Death attacked them before my eyes,
I could not oppose its bloodthirsty scythe,
Save with useless tears and sterile yearnings!
Already the flames had spread
And encircled their last retreat.
Led by the thirst for spoils,
A horde of bloodthirsty bandits,
With ax in hand opened up a passage.
O God! What horrible moments!
I thought I saw my suffering family
Between fire and murder
Beseeching vainly these brutal men,
With blades already pointed . . .
Inhuman ones! What are you doing? See their helplessness:
It is Beauty, Childhood, and Age
Who bathe with their tears your bloody arms.

O my tender friend! But this is not the moment that
I should recount the end of this deplorable scene. The
entire city was entirely ablaze. Of those who inhabited it,
some were dragged by the Negroes to the feet of the
Commissioners; a large number of them were slaughtered;
those who had saved themselves from death and slavery
were reunited on the shore, lamenting their misfortune.
What a sinister picture this part of our isle then offered!
Once a flourishing city, now reduced to ashes. These
heinous Africans, all stained with blood, were replacing
murder with excesses, amidst a population without refuge,
without clothes, and without food.

The thousands of unfortunates of different sex and

ages were sitting on the ruins of their property crying
for the loss of their families and their friends. The shore
was covered with debris, with weapons, with wounded,
with dead and with dying. On one side, a barrier of
flames and of swords; on the other, the immense expanse
of ocean. Over all was misery, want, and suffering! And
nowhere was there hope! The sun, in all its majesty, was
rising upon this baneful scene.

> O would-be philanthropists,
> Go and enjoy your works,
> Give a fraternal kiss to the cheeks
> Of those sage Congos, according to you, so misunderstood,
> And who would derive from their rights such noble usage!
> It was a glorious day when your deputy,
> In the name of your Humane Clique,
> Crying for joy, signed their liberty!
> Go then, join with your African brothers!
> There, in blood to your knees,
> Amongst the bodies of ten thousand victims
> In the rubble, the witnesses to your crimes—
> Behold them vegetate at your side,
> That stupid, indolent race
> Of your new friends, naked and dying of hunger.
> Cry, O cowardly Solons, in a triumphant voice,
> That philosophic refrain:
> " Perish the treasures of this wicked isle,
> Perish Whites and Blacks, perish the country,
> Perish the whole human race
> Rather than betray
> The Sacred Rights of Man and our precious Maxims!"

We had not determined upon our future course, and
at this time, we knew not which choice to take; whereupon
M. de Sercé, commander of the squadron, sent us word

that he was to set sail for New England and he advised us to escape with him from a country no longer inhabitable. This proposal cured our uncertainty, and we gratefully accepted the offer, which the merchant captains made, to receive us on board without payment. The vessels which were to take us had only enough provision for their crew, and we went forth to extract from the ashes any poor provisions we could find, and thus fortified, we entered the launch which they sent to carry us to the squadron.

I assure you I shed some tears; and for a long time my eyes gazed in sorrow upon my native city, over which black smoke still hovered, covering the sun. The cannon shot gave the signal for departure, the anchor was raised, the sails were set, and I was fleeing from my country without a sou—a strange experience!

> Heretofore, in foolish rapture,
> Dreaming only of frolic and pleasures,
> I imagined youth exempt of worries:
> But alas! upon that black coast,
> The Fate that saw my error
> Drew the thread of my young life
> And drenched it in the tears of sorrow,
> Yet, in spite of my misery,
> Hope wiped dry my eyes,
> And Love with a light hand
> Close to you, adorned me with flowers.
> All the blessings which I had lost,
> I could again imagine their return;
> One knows that a stormy dawn
> Often ushers in a sunny day.

I was received aboard the vessel, *Rosalie.* I was exhausted with fatigue and in need of food. My clothing, which I had not been able to change for three days, was covered with blood, sweat, and dirt, and was almost entirely in tatters; I borrowed others from the captain. Nature had given that good man dimensions and proportions very different from my own, and the clothes that he lent me made my appearance so ludicrous that they even caused some of my companions in misfortune to smile. This borrowed outfit, the only one I had then in the world, had to serve me for the entire voyage. Also, how I had lost weight! As soon as the ladies had gone to bed, I went each night on the prow and did the work of a laundryman, and enveloped myself in a sail until the breeze had dried my clothes. Sometimes, armed with a needle, I stopped the too rapid progress of much wear. I carefully guarded my hat and shoes, so that they would honor me at my debarkation.

When, not long ago, I enjoyed in Paris all the amenities of luxury, I would not have believed that one day I would be doing my laundry and mending these ridiculous clothes that had been loaned me in charity. How happy I was for several years! And then, see the constancy of Fortune!

You would like to have described, no doubt, the divers sentiments which filled my heart during the course of that voyage. I was completely ruined, without home, without money, without clothes; I was going to a country of which I knew not the language, customs, nor habits, and where I had not one person whom I could approach for assistance. I was ignorant of the fate of my family; in vain did I question for news of them among the passengers of our convoy; everyone, as I did, believed them among the number of victims.

A favorable breeze pushed us rapidly toward the continent, which was a great blessing; for, if our crossing had been even as long as the ordinary passage, we would certainly have died of hunger, considering the small amount of provisions and the number of consumers. After two weeks of hardships, boredom, and privations, we arrived in the waters of Chesapeake Bay, along the coast of Virginia. What an astounding difference there was between these shores, which the late Spring had recently embellished, and the aspect of those desolate ones which I had just left!

Yes, my sweet friend, they were there, that good and loving family, whom I thought I had lost; they were there, I saw them, and I kissed them again! Our eyes, dried out from suffering, again found tears to cry for joy; and in the happiness of the moment, we drowned all our memories of past misfortunes.

You remember the deplorable state in which I left them. Bullets were piercing their abode; burning beams were falling all around them; the inexorable swords were suspended over their heads; their prayers, their cries had been useless; with closed eyes they awaited death. All at once a chief with a ferocious air came to hasten the fatal execution. He approached with rage in his eyes, with curses on his lips, ready to watch, no doubt, and to enjoy their agony!—yet it was Heaven that sent him. He recognized my mother at first sight, whose former slave he had been. " What! it is you, my mistress," he said. " Be reassured. My soldiers will henceforth respect you and I will save you from the fury of the others—if I can." While speaking, he used a large sabre to disperse the brutes who were surrounding my family. He gave orders to a few remaining slaves to gather in haste all they possibly could. By some bizarre hazard, these useless scribblings of mine were saved from the debacle of Saint Domingue, whereas important family papers became tinder for the flames. Except for that, I am not sorry, for these words recall some moments of pleasure which memory furnishes me. Then the Congo chief, supporting my step-father and my brother-in-law, both of whom long illness had overcome, set out with his sad cortège, proceeding toward the elevated part of the Cape where were the main quarters of the Commissioners:

> What a journey, good God! for timid women,
> Like weak and weeping children,
> And men dragged, yet living,
> From beds still echoing with their sufferings!
> The tropic sun, which burns all Nature,
> Had fevered their pale brows.
> Everywhere they could see about them
> Murder, pillage, and unchecked license.
> They could hear the cries of the furious tigers
> Who were enraged to see their prey escape.
> Amongst such perils, they arrived at last
> Near dying of fatigue and sadness,
> And soon were bound in undeserving chains . . .
> O my Mother!—your son, uncertain of your fate,
> Had been swept to another shore,
> And could not avenge nor console your sufferings!
> Unfortunate captives, surrounded with horrors,
> Covered with vile tatters, and deprived of food;
> Stretched out upon the hot, hard earth;
> Seeing each instant their fierce jailors
> Come to heap upon them threats and insults.
> No doubt the sole hopes that could then console them
> Were for that refuge where no misery exists;
> And that each passing hour
> Would be for them their last!

However, the next day, by the intervention of the

chieftain, who was protecting them, they obtained permission to return to their plantation on the plain. They embarked in a skiff, but deciding to flee forever from such a forbidden country, they succeeded, by force of money and entreaties, to persuade those taking them back to steer the bark where the vessels were anchored. The signal had just been given to depart. Already several ships were moving; those that remained refused to take them under the pretext of scant provisions or of not enough space. They then sadly returned to place themselves again at the mercy of the barbarians, when the frigate, which acted as the rear guard of the convoy, saw the skiff, and at last received aboard these poor refugees. They landed at Norfolk before I did, uncertain of my fate, as I of theirs.

I will not trouble you about our transports over this unexpected reunion; you know all too well what one experiences when one finds out of danger a person for whom one has feared. I witnessed your loving sensibility, of which I, too, was the happy inspiration, when lately you made me experience those rapid transitions that carry the soul from despair to the most immoderate joy.

> With happiness I can recall
> A time dear to my heart,
> When misery and misfortune
> Delivered me, without resistance, to a cruel fever;
> I was perishing and you came to my side.
> I was wet from your burning tears,
> When your looks also spoke of grief and sorrow.
> But soon your tender caresses
> Gave back to me life, love, and desire;
> So that your kisses of rapture

Reanimated me like a sapling rose
Which the storm had nearly withered.

At Norfolk, the French, recently debarked, wandered everywhere relating their misfortunes to the sympathetic Americans. Those who had saved some money crowded the inns; the others sought out the canopies of the market-places, which gave some shelter from the inclemencies of night. I found my family already settled in a respectable inn. The large number of people who were arriving all the time created an amusing scene, however disagreeable it was for me. The mistress of the house having promised to prepare a bed for me in the parlor, I went out to see those of my friends who had escaped the carnage. It was very late when I returned and every one had retired; not wanting to disturb or awaken anyone, I entered quietly and gropingly undressed. I touched a bed; it was no doubt my own, and I threw myself upon it, whereupon I found myself seized. I wanted to escape, and I left pieces of my last garment in the hands of the ones who were pursuing me; then sharp cries resounded throughout the house, and in the trouble in which I found myself, I could not well distinguish whether they were accusing me of robbery or rape; but, I can assure you, my conscience did not reproach me of either one or the other!

Awakened by the noise, all the guests arose in haste— the door was opened and twenty candles came, all at once, to lighten up the field of battle. Imagine yourself in the center of a group of both sexes, grotesquely appareled, as they would be when they had dressed in the dark— all of them with the idea that the house was afire. In the middle of the crowd was a young man, almost naked, debating with two women. But what women . . . good

Lord! I recognized them. They were two respectable inhabitants of Saint Domingue, who settled there, I think, during the time of buccaneering. Then came the explanations; my mother being there, she assured them, while laughing, that she could attest to my good manners. The hostess asknowledged guilt at her forgetfulness in having placed others in the room she had promised me. We each made reciprocal apologies. The ladies kept their bed; and I, little tempted to dispute them, gravely gathered up my scattered clothing and went to sleep on one of the kitchen tables.

We remained one week in Norfolk, but we were told that Baltimore, being a larger city, offered more resources; and we had good need to employ ours, seeing the little money the family had been able to save in their flight. We rented a commodious boat to go up the long Chesapeake Bay; and after three days of agreeable navigation, we descended on the beautiful capital of Maryland. Here, as in Norfolk, I found singular pleasure in the strange aspect of American cities. I admired the simple but quite noble architecture of the public buildings; and the regularity of the houses, their cleanliness, their red glistening bricks separated by little white lines; the wide streets, ranged and bordered on each side by sidewalks and embellished by shade trees; the simplicity of the manners and customs; the people, hale, blooming and well-dressed. All this formed a contrast to the things I had recently seen, and to enjoy it, I wandered over all the sections of Baltimore.

One day, while walking on the wharf, I heard news of a ship that had just arrived from France full of passengers. To reach it, I had to push through a large crowd, that scemed attentive and affected. Curiosity caused me

to exert my strength, and I soon found myself near the
person who had occasioned this assembly, and to whom
all listened with much interest. Here is what it was:

A poor French exile
Who had just reached shore;
His eyes were troubled
And his voice was plaintive.
To the compassionate strangers
He was speaking of his country:

" Listen, reasonable people,
Not long ago France was
Loyal, beautiful, and quiet.
Tremble now at these furies
And weep at these sorrows!

" These seditious subjects,
Whom Hell, no doubt, inspired
With odious conspiracies,
Have lost their once great Empire,
Where both misery and terror
Have banished happiness.

" Beneath their tyrannical law
A thousand victims perished.
To love God and to serve their King,
These, to them, were crimes;
Godlessness and villainy
Are the heroes of the State.

" Delivered to contempt was
The Sovereign Majesty;
I saw the child of St. Louis
Bound with a vile chain;
I saw loyal Frenchmen
Banished from their native soil.

" Soon after, yet another crime
Dishonored our fair country;
Upon an awful scaffold
The King gave up his life.
Louis, dying as a hero,
Pardoned and pitied his executioners!

" Alas! like thy consort
Most unhappy Antoinette,
Beneath their parricidal blows
Thy august head did fall!
Thy son, our cherished hope,
How was he ravished from us!

" Almighty God, turn your eyes
Upon a people in such misery;
Protect the virtuous,
Destroy the guilty;
To the poor French exile
Give refuge and peace."

Alas! there or elsewhere, we were destined to suffer. Misfortune was as relentless to us as a raven to the victim it attacks, not leaving a moment of respite. Long illnesses, fruit of our suffering and exhaustion, assailed us all at once; and we were deprived of the consolation of being able to help one another. Thanks to my youth, I recovered, as did my sisters; my mother has remained infirm till now; my stepfather and my brother-in-law were the two victims whom death claimed. This left our family inconsolable, at the moment when we had the greatest need of their succor. They, at least, found in the tomb that furtive rest which the expatriated colonists searched for vainly from retreat to retreat, and which we, no doubt, will find only in that last one, where our friends and families have preceded us.

BALTIMORE FROM FEDERAL HILL

" After three days of agreeable navigation, we descended on the beautiful capital of Maryland. Here, as in Norfolk, I found singular pleasure in the strange aspect of American cities. I admired the simple but quite noble architecture of the public buildings; and the regularity of the houses, their cleanliness, their red glistening bricks separated by little white lines; the wide streets, ranged and bordered on each side by sidewalks and embellished by shade trees; the simplicity of the manners and customs; the people, hale, blooming and well-dressed."

FEDERAL HALL, NEW YORK CITY

"We had good friends awaiting us in New York."

So many reiterated disasters have caused to flourish in my heart a profound melancholy. I who was, not long ago, so gay, so frivolous, and so heedless, am desolate over my sorrows of the past, my misfortunes now, and those which I forebode in the obscure future.

Here I am at last at the end of this task which you imposed upon me—only still a few lines, and I will be free to leave this solitary room to which you have exiled me since this morning, at this uncomfortable desk, upon which I have leaned for several hours, scribbling with this lazy pen, which the desire to please you made me snatch from that leisure I so love.

It is for you alone that I today reopened these wounds which have almost healed. It is for you that I overcome my accustomed indolence and the repugnance I have for writing. It is for you that I have deprived myself of your presence; do I not well merit that you double your promised recompense? Ah! you will—I count upon it.

In musing thereupon my heart beats fast;
I reject that lute I find so sweet.
Discontented with my verses, wrathful Apollo
Asks, in vain, that I repolish them.
I only see, I only hear, I only seek your presence;
With copy-book beneath my arm, I quickly run
To fall before your knees.

Book Four

❦

ARGUMENT OF BOOK FOUR

The author, after the complete annihilation of his property, is left without one farthing on the continent of America and is forced to use his ingenuity to support his existence. He joins a few of his compatriots, who find themselves reduced to the same expedients, in giving concerts and balls in the small cities of the United States. These musical speculators start out for Elizabethton. Incidents of the voyage, concert, romance of the exile. Picture of a ball and different incidents which follow it. Terrifying adventure in the inn. Our reception into Society. The new Baron de Back. Experience of a good dinner which was a bad disappointment. Return of the expedition. The author, after having rested from the fatigue of this journey, recounts the events to someone who was to have gone on the same trip, but because of a slight illness had to remain in New York.

YOU had promised us, sir, to join us on a voyage to Elizabethton, but on the pretext of a migraine headache, you were not able to keep your promise. To punish you for depriving us of the advantage we had hoped to derive from your society and your talents, we have condemned you to read the account of the events which befell us upon the little Philharmonic campaign, and I am burdened with the duty of writing it to you.

You know, sir, that Thursday morning, after we were armed with a good breakfast, since soldiers of Apollo never march upon empty stomachs, with our instruments under one arm and our music under the other, we took off to the bank of the Hudson River, where twenty boat-men disputed for the honor of taking us across. We chose the smallest boat, though the least safe, in order to arrive more quickly on the other side, as we were so impatient to get off the water, that element for which musicians have much antipathy. However, our crossing was a very pleasant one.

> The sky was serene. Upon the placid waters
> Zephyrus spread his silvery wings;
> The strong movement of the restless oars
> Struck the gentle waves in even cadence
> And cast upon us jets of crystal.

While we pushed nearer to the bank our impatient bark, a crowd of idle men ran towards the shore, forming into a long line. There seemed to be an older man as leader and standing at the head of the formation, which reminded me of the serpent of the Hellespont ready to swallow up the men coming from the Trojan shore, for he set upon us an enormous spaniel, which plunged into the water to attack us. The angry beast swam around the boat the moment we tried to touch the wharf. The dog would certainly have been crushed if I had not caught it by the tail and thrown it far away, thus sacrificing the sheen of my new coat sleeve. This generous action drew a dozen " God damns "—showing the difference in attitudes of different countries;

> If the shores of this river had been
> Those of the Indus or the Ganges,
> To reward at my noble effort
> I would have obtained a Brahman plenary indulgence.

The stage awaited us at Poolshook. If you do not know what a "stage" is, let me picture for you a box of about a dozen feet long by five wide, placed upon a caisson; at equal distances, props, three feet in height, support a roof made of sapling planks, badly joined; and curtains of heavy leather fly at the will of the breeze. The sun, dust, rain, and mud penetrate the four sides without hindrance. A dozen persons of both sexes, of all colors, and of all conditions, crowd together, pell-mell, upon benches not padded nor supported by railings; trunks, baskets, boxes, etc., are off-handedly stowed under the travellers' legs—all this drawn by four stalwart horses and driven by a " driver " seated in the middle of the passengers. This "driver" is sometimes an able coachman, often a young bewildered boy, still more often, a stubborn or insolent drunk.

The country, as far as Newark, is an immense briny marsh, upon which has been laid a road of thick boards covered over with stones and sand. At high-tide water covers it all; then, heavy loads should beware, if the coachman has not the ability to guess the road he must follow. It happens sometimes (thanks to the numerous taverns) that, under pretext of allowing his horses to get a drink, he stops to have one himself.

We entered Newark, where, during the changing of horses, we drank a glass of punch and ate a half dozen " crackers." This is the custom of the country, and I highly approve of it; since, having been jolted for two hours over egregiously bumpy roads, one's breakfast has been well digested. Something of which I do not so much approve is that one must swallow with this punch and " crackers," tobacco smoke which fills the air in all the inns. Every one smokes in America; it is the general recreation. The only difference is that youth employs a cigar and age is served with a pipe. However, to vary this, they chew a " plug " from time to time; this gives the teeth a beautiful yellow effect! But, perceiving that politeness demands that one offer several swallows from his glass to a neighbor, I presented mine to a gentleman, whose costume marked him as one of the leaders of the city; for here more than anywhere else, it is the clothes that make the man.

The city of Newark stretches at least a mile along the main road, bordered by country houses, by " grocery stores," by taverns and churches—all intermingled with brush, gardens, and fields. The route to Elizabethton is very beautiful and offers for about two leagues a most pleasant countryside. It was half past two before we arrived in this last city; that was why the first words we uttered upon descending from our heavy box on wheels was an order for a large and succulent meal. The chef served us with very good fare. After thus repairing our strength, we went to look over the city. It is larger than Newark by at least one street and presents likewise a perfectly rustic setting. Cows, pigs, chickens, and horses promenaded gravely here and there between the elegant cabriolets and the heavy wagons. Some refugees from our isles had established themselves in this agreeable retreat. There were also, at this time, a number of inhabitants of New York, who came to pass the hot season, far from noise, business, and yellow fever. It was this gathering of people that fostered the idea among several ruined Creoles to come and to give a concert and ball, the receipts from which would serve to fatten their meager purses.

Upon returning from our stroll, we bent our thoughts to the large task of getting dressed. After many a hindrance we succeeded in getting costumes fine enough for a provincial fête, and we went to the field of battle.

> A ball room round in shape
> Was the place of our meeting,
> And we arrived at last
> Among the little masters of fashion.
> From antipathy or pride,
> The beauties sat apart;
> The Americans resplendent
> Were ranged on one side, alone.
> Carried away by this novelty
> We made our entrance there;
> But soon, despite their bloom
> And their imposing appearance,
> We returned to the gentleness,
> Graces, and good humor
> Of our seductive Creole girls.

All the necessary arrangements had been made by the first squadron of our musical army, who had left for New York a day ahead of us; we simply had to seize our arms and station ourselves for battle upon the stage which had been arranged at one end of the hall. This was, I believe, the first concert which had ever been given at Elizabethton. Most of the audience, taking the loud sounds which we made in tuning our instruments together for the first selection, thought M. " Iphigenia " had a strange style of composing. Then N., whom we had chosen to be our general, brandished his formidable bow, lifted his right foot, and off we went. Modesty apart, we acquitted ourselves well enough for amateurs: I was guilty of a few wrong notes, but what do you expect when there were so many pretty young ladies in the hall who made my eyes wander from the score. Your friend, M., acquitted himself with honor in his violin concerto. We had chosen a very difficult one; also, never had the Pythoness upon her sacred tripod ever made so many grimaces. His nostrils often opened like the caverns of Trophonius, and I trembled lest they swallow up R.'s flute which was at the same level. We regaled the audience with several songs in Italian, French, and English, and here is the title and the first lines of the one which your servitor, after coughing, clearing his throat, etc., rendered in his goat-like voice:

L'Exile

What brings you to the river,
Gentle troubador?
Your lute silently reposes;
Is it Love you're grieving for? etc., etc.

Precisely at ten-thirty, with the first stroke of the

fiddle's bow, the audience awakened, having slept good-naturedly during the concert. They yawned, bestirred themselves, chose partners, and the ball commenced. They started with an *anglaise*. Thirty couples, formed in two lines like soldiers in battle, jumped first upon one foot then upon the other, sometimes upon both. The arms moving as rapidly as the legs, the dancers went up and down from one end of the hall to the other, seeing nothing, reversing, dispersing all those whom they encountered on their way. This little exercise lasted for about one hour, and always to the same tune. Then they retired to the buffet, where everyone according to his taste took either beer or punch, and cakes. They then repaired their disordered attire; the men, armed with little colored silk handkerchiefs, wiped the perspiration from their faces and the dust from their clothes; the ladies, with little pocket combs, smoothed their disarranged hair.

After the long and tiring anglaise, they prepared for a quadrille which here they call a cotillion. Our worthy dancing master! what would have been your indignation if you could have seen with what mockery the Americans treat our graceful though difficult steps. They believe that only an idiot walks with feet pointed outward, or performs an *entrechat* or a *simpole*. I gained the good graces of three or four young ladies by my conversation, but a fatal pirouette, which I had the misfortune to make in one of the dances, caused me to lose their fancy.

But this event was not the most disastrous one of the evening. A French beauty with whom I was dancing tried a figure which ended in her falling down. It was my fault; yielding myself entirely to the pleasure of admiring the charms of my partner, I forgot to extend my arms at the proper moment to hold her. Imagine my despair. The next day I wrote and sent her a little poem, very humbly offering my apologies, explaining my forgetfulness of the moment, and assuring her that her tumble only revealed more of her grace and beauty. The modest tumbler claimed that my complimentary picture of the incident was quite wrong, and that she had fallen as modestly as possible; which made me feel obliged to send her the verification of a dozen witnesses, that her garters were rose colored (and trimmed with blue).

Toward the end of the ball the French demanded a waltz. While it was being danced, all the matrons covered their eyes with their hands. I think, however, that their fingers were not very close together. By Jove! One does not trifle here with decency. A young lady can properly go out with a young man until midnight and run about everywhere without her mother; but *waltz*—for shame!

At present, Sir, if you are curious to know my opinion of the ladies who were at the ball, I will say that Madame I. seemed to me the most beautiful; Madame T., the prettiest; Mademoiselle B., the loveliest; and Mademoiselle d'E., the best dancer.

Our spirits were prepared for an entire night of debauchery, so we had ourselves served an American supper; that is to say, oysters in butter, beefsteak and Madeira wine, over which we gaily employed ourselves and did not think of going to bed until about 4 o'clock— to dream of all manner of things! We were awakened by an extraordinary loud noise which was succeeded by deafening wails. First, as a result of my dream, I thought M. X. was entering, sword in hand, but I found in my arms only my pillow; then, I thought I was still in Saint Domingue, and I jumped out of bed crying, " To arms! " I thought the Negro monsters were in the house; I thought the city on fire, I thought . . . I know not what; it was simply that one of our roommates was making unprecedented efforts in getting from under his bed. His cot had upset. I do not know why, but he found himself so choked in his feather-bed and coverlets that we had much trouble in quieting him.

We had been engaged to spend the next day at the home of Madame P. We arrived at noon and we found a number of guests. M. P., whose character has much affinity with that of Baron de Back, proposed right away to play a quartet before dinner. We gave him the honor of playing the violin. In a difficult allegro passage of Mozart, the enthusiastic virtuoso was trying as hard as the Devil; his arm went up and down with the rapidity of a wood-chopper; the sweat was falling from his forehead in large drops. All at once he called out in a terrible voice: " Gentlemen, it is not right! Gentlemen, someone has lost his place!" Everyone laughed till he cried; it was himself, who, in the excitement of playing, had passed his bow between the strings and the body of his instrument, and was pulling and pushing with full strength without perceiving his blunder.

I presumed that the principal motive of the invitation we had received was with the idea that we could amuse the company with our talents; also that I was doubly welcomed for the reputation I had in making others laugh by recounting stories in the manner of Thilmot.

For the rest, Sir, we cannot complain of our journeys. We had had music, dancing, fine food, exquisite wines, gracious welcomes, innocent games, and a few kisses here and there. In gratitude, each of us paid his share, in trying his best to give pleasure.

After a delicious little supper,
Where the Bordeaux was not scarce,
All separated to get some needed rest.
Our squadron of musicians
Sang along the road
With a guitar as our accompaniment.
Alas! to our sweetest sounds
The Americans only replied
By casting stones upon us;
Here, 'twould seem for music they care not much!

They gave as pretext for this hospitality that they wanted to sleep; however, we were more sleepy than they, I assure you, yet that did not prevent us from singing; so according to that, you can easily see that they were in the wrong! Upon my word, I thought for a moment we would have to display our skill as pugilists. This process is most utilized here, as the manner of settling dissensions; and gentlemen themselves do not abstain therefrom; they even allow children to have fist fights, and look upon this little amusement as very reasonable. One day, I presumed to rush to separate two lads who were already bloody from fighting, and the spectators, who formed a large circle around these gladiators, told me not to meddle in other peoples' affairs, and several assumed the attitude of wanting to blacken my eye or break my nose.

This night passed without further incident, and we all slept like egoists who had supped well. Our dreams reflected the quarrel of the previous night, and hardly had Dawn opened, with rosy fingers, the gates of the Orient, than we awakened in the most belligerent of humors. Soon we were fighting each other with pillows, covers, shoes, etc., which ended in a half dozen broken windows, and counted for dead were two pillows and one counterpane. But, being generous heroes, we made indemnity to the owners of the battlefield for the ravages made by our army.

We intended leaving for New York after breakfast, but the stage was so full that we were obliged to wait for the one leaving in the afternoon. After the flattering remarks made to us by our hosts of the past evening, we thought we might appear at their door informally, hoping to be invited to remain for dinner. As a consequence, we presented ourselves and inquired whether they desired to engage us again that day or, at least, whether M. X. would like to play again with our quartet, since we had been unable to board the crowded morning bus and had to wait for the late one. To our astonishment and disappointment, they did not ask us to remain for dinner, as we had hoped after our praising the richness of Madame's sauces, the lightness of her tarts, and the thickness of her cream. Having played awhile, we stopped our music, saying we must leave, as the driver would soon be over at the inn. With flat stomachs, but hopeful air, we returned to our hostelry to partake of roast-beef dripping with blood, unglazed ham, chicken swimming in grease, half-raw potatoes, badly cooked vegetables, and heavy pastry.

The evening stage stopped in front of the inn, and it was again already filled. However, as the disappointments we had experienced that day caused us to feel antipathy towards Elizabethton, we demanded places. We were refused, and being in a bad humor, we insisted. They became angry. At last, after several verbal skirmishes,

Into the defenceless stage
We entered with war-drums beating.

The garrison, already full,
Could scarce receive us.
I slipped gently between a
Young Negress, going to market, and a lean Quaker,
Whose bony arms seemed to pierce my clothes.
M. B., too large for the coach's bench,
Had his full-moon-like posterior
Resting on projecting baggage
And his wide shoulders forced
Against the bosom of a mother.
M. E., three inches too tall,
Sat with bowed back
As if holding up the firmament;
And R. T., up in front,
Was collecting in the flight
The mud-splashings
From our trotting equipage.
We had, besides all this,
The sad whistling of the wind
That through our stage coach blew,
And the noise of the falling
Waters from the clouds descending;
And thunder, finally, to complete
This tumult, brought its deafening noise.

Judge, Sir, of our impatience to end our journey. This impatience did not hasten, however, the speed of our laden carriage; and all the cursing of the driver, the efforts of the horses, and the wishes of the passengers were useless on roads upon which a tempest had descended and rendered almost impassable.

It was ten o'clock that night when we reached the shore of the Hudson River. We found the crossing very different from the one on the day of our departure. A number of our companions decided to spend the night in

Poolshook. But we who are now used to accustom ourselves to brave death, under whatever form it menaces
us, had good reasons to like neither the beds nor the meals
of the inn; we who needed to protect a purse already too
flattened; we, particularly, who had good friends awaiting
us in New York, took our courage in hand and jumped
into a boat, and were transported safe and sound to the
opposite shore, where we were complimented by some for
our daring and blamed by others for our imprudence.

> Here, presented from our little voyage,
> Are its principal events:
> You will see that, as usual, there were
> Some pleasures and some misfortunes.
> But the greatest distress we had,
> I assure you, in the name of us all,
> Was the absence of a friend.

Book Five

❦

ARGUMENT OF BOOK FIVE

The Spaniards had taken from the Negroes the city of Fort Dauphin, and their intention was to take possession of the whole island, they said, in the name of the King of France. They had spread, on the American continent, proclamations in which they entreated all the Creoles of Saint Domingue to come to their aid in this noble endeavor. I decided to leave. Sea voyage. Our reception. Picture of the island at the time of my arrival. Details of the horrible massacre of the French in the city of Fort Dauphin. What happened to me and especially the manner in which I escaped. Reception in Môle St. Nicholas and departure for Jérémie. How I arrived in St. Marc and in Arcahaye, which was under the authority of the English, and took up duty.

Picture of Port-au-Prince and the life which they lead there. During the idleness of camp life I write this, and I address it to my sister, who thinks me among the number of victims of the massacre of Fort Dauphin.

Camp Bizoton, Saint Domingue

[JUNE 1795]

MY sister, dry your tears, recall your past gaiety, it is
I who write you, I, your well-loved brother, the companion of your childhood; I, whom you saw leave with
much regret, whose cruel and premature death you have
grieved for a year.

Yes, I still exist and yearn to see you and to forget the
long train of sorrows which almost overpowered me, and
which I will try to recount to you. Sheltered upon the
hospitable shores of the United States of America, I consoled myself in the bosom of my family for the past
misfortunes of my youth. I lived in poverty, no doubt,
but the presence of those whom I loved rendered me
less sensitive to the caprices of blind destiny. That
time of comparative good fortune was of short duration.
There appeared in all cities on the American continent,
a proclamation by the Spanish General, Don Garcias de
Moreno, couched in the most pleasing terms and full of
the most noble promises. It entreated the Creole fugitives
to come and rally under the flag of His Catholic Majesty—
in order to help the generous Castilians wrest from the
Negroes the important colony of Saint Domingue and to
return it to France.

Notwithstanding the ties that bound me to Baltimore,
I had to leave; duty, honor, vengeance, alas! want itself—
all forced me to this measure. I finally embarked, at the
end of May on an American schooner whose living quarters encompassed twelve feet square! The modesty of

our finances did not permit us to choose a larger boat. And, despite our cramped situation, my comrades expressed only gladness, and reproached me unceasingly for the sorrow that I could not help but show.

Contrary winds detained us for several days in the superb Chesapeake Bay, whose entire banks showed cultivation and offered picturesque scenes. We were obliged to tack from side to side, and at times to anchor at the mouth of several little rivers to await the breeze or the tide. At these times we would alight on the shore to take another farewell to this beautiful temperate zone, which we were leaving perhaps forever. We gathered beneath cool shade trees; we picked fragrant strawberries, which covered the fields; we drank long draughts of nectar which the errant streams benignly let us steal. The "countrymen" from neighboring cottages assembled, and we recounted our deplorable adventures. They, touched no doubt by so much misfortune in an age so peaceful, brought quantities of cabbages, green peas, potatoes, and chickens—

> A great pity, 'tis certain,
> To spoil this charming picture,
> But truth does here command it.
> Alas! you should have seen
> Us poor travelers with arms extended,
> Eager and grateful for these offerings,
> And how the brusque and heartless
> Countrymen snatched them away —
> All those precious vegetables and fowls!
> "You think them gifts? Well, bless our souls!"
> They said. "You must remember
> That here as elsewhere on our soil
> No money means, by God, no food!"

At these words of insult, we reached hurriedly for our purses, but finding them empty, we returned aboard, taking back with us only our appetites made greater by our excursions.

In spite of everything, it was to these little promenades that we owed the sole agreeable moments of our voyage. Our greatest affliction was a perilous sea, which tossed about our puny bark. Sitting on the bridge, clinging as best I could to the rigging, I laughed and trembled by turn at the spectacle I was witnessing. Some of the passengers were making unbelievable grimaces in efforts to vomit. Others sang, accompanied by the whistling of the wind and by the music of the cases fastened to the bridge. The sailors cursed, the captain, half drunk, screamed like a maniac and grumbled at everyone; then came an enormous wave roaring upon us, covering the boat, which succeeded in silencing the cries of terror.

One night, when I was engulfed in a profound first sleep, dead to past pains and living in happy dreams, I was awakened with a start by a frightful noise. There was much going and coming, pulling of ropes, hoisting or lowering of sails. Everyone was talking, crying, and cursing at once. I ran to the bridge, and I saw not far away the prettiest little rock that ever crushed a boat. My faith! Our boat was going straight ahead, despite all the attempts of our captain, who was already trembling at being obliged to put water in his wine. Fortunately for us, a French Marine officer was among the passengers. He took command and brought us into harbor without touching those terrible crags, where your poor brother would doubtless have been the food of fishes.

The day after this little adventure, we saw the sea-coast covered with mangrove trees, where Nature had hidden the entrance to Fort Dauphin. We anchored after going through a long narrow canal, defended by numerous batteries, which made the city impenetrable by sea. As soon as we cast anchor, a troop of *alguasils* came aboard and announced that we would have to wait to disembark until they obtained permission from His Excellency, the General Don Garcias. Unfortunately for us, this Don Garcias was then absent from the city. He was at the head of the army, braving the most formidable perils, and winning victories in the field of battle which would immortalize him—so they said.

This is why we had to remain for three days on our floating prison, exposed to mosquitoes which gathered from us the fresh blood we had brought from the North. At last the new Cortés arrived. This indomitable conquerer had great courage to lead twelve hundred men against the Fort of Jaquezi, which was defended by fifty men; and after spending several days in cautious maneuvers, his humanity surpassing his valor, he decided to spare his enemies, and, in consequence, he led his army back safe and sound—that is to say, almost so, but for a few lost through fever during the course of the promenade.

We soon received orders from His Excellency, and the launch deposited us upon that sad part of the shore which I had left about twelve months before, under deplorable circumstances. There we found the soldiers, thin, dirty, and ragged. We were placed amongst them in grave, silent, and slow fashion by an old officer who carried a parasol in place of a sword. As the Spanish are never in haste, I had time to cast a glance over the surroundings and upon the groups near by. What was my surprise, O God! when I beheld that this hoard of Negroes, who had brought steel and fire to our unfortunate country, had become allies of the King of Spain! These former brigands were dressed in all manner of bizarre accoutrements, remnants from their pillaging; some wore the upper portions of magnificent costumes, with neither pants nor stockings, while some had on cassocks or petticoats. I could not help smiling despite my rage at their carnival-like and grotesque clothing.

We were escorted to headquarters. The General was having his siesta, as was his entire suite, and we had to wait until these gentlemen awakened. At last we saw them yawning and rubbing their eyes; first the aides, then the secretaries, after them the chaplains, followed by the confessor, Father Vasquez. To terminate the procession His Excellency, himself, came to. The ceremony began with the sign of the cross, which was succeeded by an invocation to Our Lady of Seven Sorrows. We were subjected to long interrogations; we were asked if we believed in the Holy Trinity, the infallibility of the Pope, the souls in purgatory, etc., etc.

Although we were called upon to aid in winning back our country—our firearms were taken from us, and even our knives. There, while making the sign of the cross, we promised fealty, and for the last act of this ceremony, we were made to kiss an old quarto which we were assured was the Holy Scripture.

Returning from this audience, I saw the wounded of the army back from its brilliant expedition. In place of medicine, the sick and wounded were surrounded by confessors, and made to kiss relics, or were covered with scapulars. It was a singular spectacle, this crowd of monks, bearded, beardless; with shoes, without shoes; shorn, unshorn; in grey, red, black, white, blue, green;

walking armed with rosaries, guns, and flags. Never had I seen a collection so large and varied.

Fort Dauphin is situated fourteen leagues * from Cap Français. Its distance from the Spanish frontier is, I believe, eight leagues † by way of Monté Christ and four leagues ** by way of Dajabón. The city is fairly large, well constructed, and divided into large, straight, though unpaved, streets. There were several public buildings with large fountains; a river ran near its walls. The large quantity of swamp-lands nearby rendered the air unhealthy; this is a matter which could be easily remedied, and then the city, by its advantageous situation and its port facilities, could become the finest in Saint Domingue. The plain on which it depends for food is immense and very fertile.

Before our troubles, Fort Dauphin, despite the unhealthiness of its climate held a considerable population and formed the commercial center for the French and Spanish provinces. Since my arrival, I have found it almost deserted and destitute of all that could be useful or agreeable. Also, how slowly the days seemed to pass! Bad food, boring society, monotonous walks, processions, funerals, the siesta, chocolate to drink, Divine Service twice a day—thus were my hours filled.

Eight days had hardly elapsed since my arrival at Fort Dauphin, when the infected air of this city attacked me, and soon a malignant fever carried me to death's door. How I then longed for the presence of my family! Soon after my illness the disastrous day arrived, when, betrayed by the laws of honor and of humanity, the Spanish

* 38.64 miles.
† 20.68 miles.
** 11.04 miles.

delivered swords to the Negroes. The innocent French victims whom they had petitioned to return, they now prepared to sacrifice. The act was premeditated, there is no doubt on that point. So that no one could escape, we were confined to the city. So that nothing could retard the fatal execution, our firearms were taken from us. So that our blind confidence would make us be at hand and prevent our trying to escape, we were promised solemnly that our arms would be returned to us the next day, and then we would march on the enemy. After a few days, several characteristic alarms were circulated through the city. The Negroes showed increased insolence. All the officers of merit withdrew, one after another, and under different pretexts.

The native, Juan Sanchez, left with the public funds— at last Don Garcias Moreno himself went to Monte Christ, leaving the command to Cassasola, an officer both old and stupid. The only officer of note who remained with us was Colonel Francisco de Montalvo. He was thought to be too honorable a man to let into the secret, and his presence caused us all to put away the idea of treason.

On the 7th of July, 1794, I was again forced to go to bed because of the weakness which accompanies convalescence. One day there was a movement and an extraordinary noise which made me jump up in haste to look for the cause. It was the Black auxiliary army of Spain marching in file towards the big Square. The regular troops, in battle array before their barracks, received them with full honors, notwithstanding the fact that it was agreed in a treaty that they would never be allowed to enter the city.

I saw at last the famous Jean François, this monster

127

who is renowned for countless crimes. Mounted on a
fiery steed, he was leading the army. The splendor of
jewels and the high polish of silver rendered his black,
wrinkled skin and gross features more hideous. Upon
his thick kinky hair the martial helmet stood up clumsily.
The sword which had caused so much blood to flow was
hanging by his side, and the hypocrite had placed upon
himself, among military decorations, rosaries and sacred
medals. With a holy air he led his murderous hordes,
counting on the protection of the fierce Castilians who
filled the city. A group of Frenchmen whom this spectacle
allured followed the procession, I amongst them, trailing
in fascination. On the field the troops were placed in
battle formation; the chief looked about him, and then
mounting a large rock, with a wild look and sonorous
voice, he addressed his disheveled brutes.

As you understand the Creole Negro's dialect, I prefer
to give you his discourse as he spoke it, so you can better
judge his singular eloquence. Here it is, word for word:
" Listen all of you who have fought together with me;
do you remember what I told you in the wood? " " Yes,
yes, General," responded the Negroes, all the while preparing their arms. " Well then " he said, " get going,
all of you! Slay every one, slaughter each of them as
you would a hog; listen to no cries of mercy! "

After this harangue, the Congos all responded with
horrible shrieking. Then vomiting forth thousands of
imprecations against the French, and crying: " Long live
the King of Spain! "—they dashed out in all directions,
striking, slaughtering all they could reach. The Whites
who escaped the first discharge of musket fire ran like
lightning; and danger gave me for the moment enough
strength to follow. Bullets whistled by my ears; my

clothes were pierced; at each instant one of my companions was mortally wounded. At last my strength gave out; the enemy was closer and his blows more certain. I can still see one terrible face with projecting forehead and hollow cheeks, his sunken red eyes presaging horror, his immense pale mouth emitting fury. His skin was covered with many bizarre carvings, marks of dignity among his barbarous people. In his strong hand he held a heavy hammer. His gesture, his look, and even his smile said, " You are to die! " How can I recount for you what I experienced in that last moment! He was upon me. This was the end! I was alone, unarmed, and being at the end of my strength, had fallen. He seized me, was ready to kill. I was only stunned by the hammer-blow which he gave me—happily for me, these Negroes were eager to chase those who were running to get away and they were not, at that moment, ready to amuse themselves in despoiling and mutilating their victims.

I do not know how long I remained between life and death. When I did begin to regain consciousness, I was utterly confused. I could hardly see and I did not know who or where I was, nor what had occurred to me. Blood was coming from my nose and mouth which I wiped off mechanically, having no idea what it could be. Soon, clarity and memory returned, and I was shivering and a few tears escaped from my eyes. I arose slowly and with pain, and looking about me, I saw that I was surrounded by bodies and a few wounded men dragging themselves to some obscure corner. I heard screams from neighboring streets of those being massacred; I heard the noise of the breaking open of houses to drag out their inhabitants. Then came the cries of more cannibals and bullets

announcing the approach of other murderers. Not far
away was a Spanish barracks to which I dragged myself.
I fell at the feet of some officers and asked for assistance
in the name of God and humanity. This was in vain;
my helplessness, with blood still running from my mouth,
my wounded head, and my death pallor did not touch
them. I managed to say, " Brave and generous Castil-
lians, in pity give a gun, that I may at least die a soldier
if I must lose my life to those monsters who want to
take it away." They did not even deign to answer. "Well,
then," I cried out, " kill me, kill me yourselves; your
inconceivable cold blood will prevent me from languishing
beneath their blows." They were deaf to all my entreaties.
I lunged toward one of them to pull away his sword;
the others surrounded me and pushed me down with
their gun butts. Who would believe that, at that same
instant, these inhuman soldiers stopped abruptly at the
sound of the Angelus ringing and turned their faces
toward the skies to murmur sacrilegious prayers! I got
to my feet as quickly as my weakness would allow, and
fled from street to street, pursued by bullets. I looked
everywhere for a friend, a place of shelter or protection,
but I found only assassins, Spaniards, other victims in
flight, and the dead. In a few minutes more, two young
men met me and we joined in helping each other. We
went into an empty courtyard, then climbed to an attic,
but unfortunately we were seen by several Negroes.
While they were trying to open the courtyard gate, they
saw where we were. They fired, but missed; then they
began to climb to our last retreat. We seemed lost without recourse. In vain did I look over the attic, but could
see no way out. I was in despair, when Providence cast
my eyes upon a trap-door! Hope gave me strength to

manage to lift the heavy trap, and not worrying about how far I would fall or where I would find myself, I opened it and let myself drop. I was in a well-furnished room. A young and pretty lady was seated near a table, her head leaning upon her right hand and her left hand holding a handkerchief with which she was wiping her eyes, no doubt weeping for some dear one who had been killed. At the sound of my fall, the young lady uttered a lamentable cry and fainted. I wished to revive her, to reassure her, but I heard the voices of the brigands who had reached the attic. My two companions were following my lead and fell into the room at the moment that I was crawling under a huge bed. Alas! The Negroes quickly followed through the same trap-door, seized the two victims, and without regard to their entreaties, cut them to pieces and strewed the room with their remains. They then went over to the lady, who began to show signs of regaining consciousness. She hardly saw them as her bewildered eyes turned to the terrible objects which surrounded her.

The beasts began by tearing off the jewels which she had on her person; then they betook themselves to satisfy their brutal lust. What scenes of horror and cruelty! I could see her lying amidst the human debris, pale, immobile. I could see the excited Africans, disputing the right for the first ebony embrace of her tender beauty. The monsters! Their desire resembled rage, what with their glistening teeth and wild expressions. At that moment they were stopped by the great noise of a new horde who had forced entrance into the house; then the chief entered and prevented the last outrage. Perhaps he thought her worthy to be reserved for himself, as he cried, " Comrades, what are you doing? You abandon

yourselves to pleasures while there still remain a number
of Whites to slaughter? Leave this woman. You can be
sure of finding her again tonight." At his words the wild
horde became more avid for blood than lust, and they
hurled themselves into the street. A short time later the
young lady revived. A terrible thought came to her
mind, no doubt, as she finally became conscious of her
position and of her disordered clothes, for I heard her
burst into most terrible sobs. Feeble and despairing, she
dragged herself into a closet, the door of which was hid
by a tapestry.

You cannot conceive what I experienced during these
different scenes. At times I trembled with horror, at
times I wept in despair—there were moments when it
seemed I wanted to die; and perhaps, had I a weapon,
I would have prevented those beasts the trouble of trying
to kill me. At other moments existence seemed dear to
my timid heart; then, the least noise would make me
quake, and I would believe that I was taking my last
breath. I imagined another blood-thirsty horde would
find me and mingle my members with those others in the
horrible scene which was before my eyes. Every few
minutes new bands of Negroes entered the room; some
looked about and thought there was nothing further for
them to accomplish. Some mutilated further the human
remnants, solely for the pleasure of destruction; others
sat on the bed, which alone hid me from their eyes, and
would recount to each other their exploits of the day.
They counted the number of victims who had fallen
beneath their blows, the method which they used in their
slaughterings. They laughed at the agonies they inflicted
with their torments, and complained that they could not
find more Whites on whom to vent their rage.

It was in this deplorable situation that I remained from midday until seven at night. During this period of misery I could never find occasion to speak to my companion. At last, at twilight, the unfortunate one, hearing no more noise, took this advantage to leave her closet. I called her in a weak voice and explained to her how I happened to be there and what had transpired since my arrival. " I was a witness to your dangers," I told her; " let me reassure your frightened heart that you came through unharmed." She then wished to get to the brigand leader, whose wife had been her slave in happier days. She promised to send a patrol to fetch me, which she flattered herself able to obtain, and after giving me a large pitcher of water, she quietly left the house.

A little later more Negroes came in; they were furious at not finding anyone to kill and wondered what had happened to a number of Whites still unfound who were on their list of victims. Finding nothing more to pillage in the room but the bed under which I was, they resolved to take it, and set about the task of doing so. Imagine my state at the moment. All my blood seemed to freeze and my limbs shook with terror. Already they were taking the mattress; then they began to dismantle the bed. I vainly hoped not to be seen in the shadows of near night and remained immobile and glued against the wall, but they saw me.

They seized me with barbaric acclamations. They tore at my clothing, they dragged me by the hair, by the legs and arms, into the street in front of the house, where a circle of cannibals formed about me, crying banefully, " Kill him, kill him!" Their swords, bayonets, and hatchets were uplifted. I closed my eyes, was mute and nearly unconscious, awaiting the signal for the final blow.

A patrol of Negroes arrived; the leader rushed up, extricated me, and dispelled the assassins, forbidding them in the General's name to harm anyone, but giving orders to put in prison all those who had escaped massacre.

I could hardly stand, and two Negro men were obliged to help me walk. We had to move slowly and were often interrupted. It was clear to see that it was with regret that they had to do me this service and to obey the new order they had received. The streets through which they took me were littered with the dead. By the moon's pale light I was trying to see some of the victims who might be my friends, but the ground was covered mostly by their torn and bleeding bodies.

Profoundest darkness reigned in the prison where I was thrown. I spent the night overwhelmed by fatigue, want, and most cruel thoughts. All contributed to redouble my melancholy. A storm arose, and the thunder roared and resounded in echoes among the neighboring mountains. Gun shots, from time to time, announced new victims. About me I could hear the cries of misery and of pain from the terrible injuries of cruelty. I felt stifled by the unendurable heat; sometimes I dragged myself near the door to catch a breath of the cooler air from without, and my ferocious jailors forced me back with kicks. At times I lay upon the ground, my head resting on my arms, desolate and cursing my existence. At other times I became more tranquil and resigned myself to my fate; I even became sufficient master of my senses to entertain my Muse with my suffering, and here is a romance which I remember composing during one of these moments:

> Still so young, I have known much misery,
> And also sorrow to poison my days.

Alas! This wretched life,
Why should it be so prolonged?
The sweet hours of my childhood
Promised me a radiant future.
Vain prediction! 'Twas useless
To hope; I was born only to suffer—
Farewell, Happiness, upon whose dawn I was just entering,
Farewell Pleasure, which I so little knew.
Of dear things past, there is left to me
Only regret to have lost them so soon!
Family, friends, and my understanding Love,
All tender objects whom I cherish!
May Heaven spare their lives and vouchsafe them
Happy days which I had hoped to share.

Thus absorbed in my thoughts, I did not perceive the sun's first rays which began to lighten the horrors of my prison. I was called from my reverie by the affectionate voice of a lady who recognized me lying there, called me by name and tried to console me. It was your friend, the young Mme. de B. Alas! She had more need of consolation than I. I saw her still stained with the blood of her husband whom they slaughtered in her arms, and her ears were still bleeding from having their ornaments torn from them. She was indeed to be pitied! Hardly sixteen, sweet and lovely, she was without succor among monsters who respected nothing. Besides having lost her friends, as I had, she had the sorrow of losing that one whom her heart had chosen to be the companion of her happiness and sorrow, and whom she had seen taken by a dreadful and premature death.

Seeing her pale, bleeding, and disheveled, and yet with a tender voice trying to calm my sorrowing soul, I ceased crying over my sufferings, which had seemed so cruel,

135

to cry with her over her own in this place where we both were imprisoned.

What a sinister sight the prison offered! I saw desolate women, half-naked images of terror and despair. Some carried the tender fruit soon to be born, only to grieve always for a lost father. Some presented in vain to their nurslings breasts that were lacerated from twenty-four hours of infant restlessness. I saw men covered with wounds imploring vainly for help. Some still wore women's clothes by which they thought to escape the murderers.

I must have been a horrible sight. Imagine a long skeleton covered with torn clothes, and from head to foot in sweat, blood, and mud. All morning the Negroes came in crowds to insult us in our distress. They made us hear clearly that they intended us to die in torture. Consequently, during the hottest part of the day, a detachment prodded us with gun-butts, and led us to the place where criminals were executed.

Starting upon this awful procession, I faced the end without turning pale. I was sick and despairing and death would be a pleasure. But, nearing the impious altar for innocent victims, I rediscovered in my heart all the bonds that made life dear, and I found tears falling upon my cheeks. Hardly had we arrived at our destination, when from fatigue I fell almost dying on the ground. Fever which had never left me, lack of nourishment, and the sun, which poured its fire on my uncovered head, took from me the little reason which I had preserved until then. I have only an imperfect notion of what happened to me during the fifteen days that followed. I do not know why they did not massacre me. It seemed that a bit later a white man, on horseback and decorated with the Cross of St. Louis, came to announce that we had been pardoned. It seemed that I was carried from house to house, by whom I do not know, and I ignored the reason why. It seemed that some persons took pity on my situation and put me in a place of safety.

When reason returned, I found myself lying on a stretcher in what looked like a Negro's cabin. At my side sat a young Negress, a former servant of my family. She told me that those who had survived the massacre had been given orders to leave the country. At her behest, a chief, whose wife she was, had me brought to his house, and she had nursed me. She warned me to remain hidden, for, despite the order given by Jean François, Whites were still being assassinated in the streets; and she assured me that she would make the necessary arrangements to procure for me a passage on an American ship. In fact, a few days later I found the means, thanks to her, of getting aboard a schooner which was leaving for Môle St. Nicholas.

There I met some of my companions in danger. Some had run to the seacoast, where yawls rescued them and brought them into the basin. Others had the good fortune to find undiscovered shelters. Some of them impersonated faithful servants. A large number, by chance, got to the place where the regiment of the Marquis de Montalvo was having a battle. It seemed that this officer wanted to march against the Negroes, but orders from a superior forced him to remain at his post. He saved, at least, all those who got to him. As for the fugitives who were found that night and put in prison, why they were spared is something that I do not know.

> Here, my sister, is the sad story
> Of my voyage to Fort Dauphin.

Ah! The many horrors which I saw
Can hardly be believed;
But I was both an actor and witness,
And suffering caused that
All be engraved upon my memory.
You can see those young Frenchmen,
Brave companions of your brother,
Only thinking of success and glory,
Who left with happy laughter
The shores of hospitable America.
Eight hundred of these lads are dead,
Delivered to voracious animals;
And the scattered and confusèd few
Leave scarce a trace behind!
Those who by happy chance
Escaped the dagger's point
Will go, like me, some place on earth,
To tell, no doubt, their friends
About these same deplorable events
As I have just been telling you.
While implacable Death
Under a thousand disguises
Used his sharp scythe
To reap us down with little effort,
An entire army remained inert,
Viewing it all complacently.
And those renowned Castilians,
So full of honor and of valor,
Even in the midst of their own ranks
Allowed the defenseless slaughter
Of those who through false promises
Returned at their beseeching!

They tried to palliate their crime by saying they had
been informed that we wanted to revolt against them and
deliver that part of the island to the English, who were

already in possession of other parts. Another excuse given was that Jean François, outraged at the return of the French proprietors, threatened to start a rebellion of all the Negroes against the Spanish, unless he was promised that we would be delivered to him to be done with as he chose. Ridiculous excuses! As if a handful of disarmed Frenchmen could seize a city where the Spanish had three or four thousand soldiers, supported besides by a fleet of ships. We demanded arms insistently, it is true; but only because we had come to recapture our country. If they had not called us under this pretext, we would have taken care not to have left the tranquil shores of rich and safe North America to come to languish and perish in an ancient city full of poverty and filth.

As to the warriors of Jean François, one would have to be very cowardly to fear them. I saw his army pass by. It did not contain a thousand men, and all were poorly armed. We had only to be regimented and charged to fight them, and their army would soon have ceased to exist. Furthermore, had it been true that our presence in Fort Dauphin had become harmful and dangerous, it would have been very simple to have rid themselves of the threat. They could have arrested us; even chained us and sent us back to the places whence they had us come. But no! The Spanish know only how to use knives. The monsters!

Ah! the memory is graven in my heart
Of that day, that long and awful day of suffering!
When, pale and desolate, fainting from weakness,
Covered with sweat, dirt, and blood,
In a plaintive voice I told them of my misery.
I was at their feet, and I was there in vain!
Ah! may you soon, degenerate people,

Hear resound the hour of vengeance!
May the soldiers of France
Invade, one day, your dishonorable soil,
And hurl upon your degraded race
The wrongs you made us suffer!
In centuries to come
May all learn of your perfidy,
And learn also that Heaven took charge of the punishment.

In two days I arrived at Môle St. Nicholas. It is quite a pretty little city, built at the foot of the mountains and situated on a bay which forms the best and largest port of the colony. The squadron found shelter there from winds and enemies; and found in the immense stores all they needed for provisions. The city is very healthful. Spring water runs in the streets, where they have planted trees whose heavy foliage offers an agreeable shade; and a portion they call the Gorge is a delightful promenade. Nearly all houses have gardens which furnish an abundant supply of vegetables and fruits. The grapes and figs in particular are better than those of France. The country is not suitable for the cultivation of produce for export, and so there is little commerce in Môle. It is mainly a harbor for our French war ships. I found it in the possession of the English who received the Creole fugitives with much respect and generosity.

As I had no means and as I was still too weak to make my living by working, I resolved to ask hospitality from one of my relatives, well established in Jérémie, a province almost intact, of which the English had become masters and drew therefrom very large resources.

I had another attack of fever while on board, and there was no one who could care for me, and no medicine to help me get well. The captain, who was very much concerned at my situation, had the goodness to stop at St. Marc, in order to get rid of me; and he deposited me without ceremony on shore, where he abandoned me to my star. Lying on the burning sand, a myriad of insects tormented me but to my great good fortune I saw the face of one of my old college friends. Under the generous and tender help he offered, I took hope. He took me to a superb sugar plantation which he owned in Arcahaye. This rich plain, with the mountains that surrounded it, was one of those privileged spots which the revolt and fire had not yet reached; but I was exposed to a danger even greater, perhaps, than those I had yet experienced.

I fell into the hands of an Aesculapius, who did not invent gunpowder, but who prided himself on being the inventor of a remedy that could combat all maladies. For a long time M. Purgon had searched for an occasion to try out his Balm, which some called his Poison. At any rate, I became his man, and if his cure did not succeed, my depleted condition and death could be attributed to Nature! I will leave it to a higher faculty to decide if it was due to Art or Nature that I owed the terrible developments of my illness. I was often in delirium; I laughed, sang, and cried by turn. Often I arose at night, evading the vigilance of my guards, and ran over the plantation. I devoured all the food that I came upon, whatever it was; at other times, I gave forth loud cries, I knocked on all the doors, I awoke everyone, I complained that the King of Spain would not give me my bed. Often they found me in the morning, lying unconscious in a cane-brake, or stretched out in one of the brooks by which the property was watered. My doctor finally decided to suspend his medicine and to abandon me to Nature. In a few weeks I regained my reason, my health, and my strength!

I then learned that the government had permitted the Chevalier de P. to raise a legion of Africans, whose officers would be well known Whites and accustomed to the climate. I hastened to the Colonel and told him all that had happened to me; he received me with the greatest kindness and gave me a lieutenancy. As the war which we were waging was one in which rapid advancement was possible, I soon was made commander of a company. Notwithstanding my new position, I did not find myself comfortable all at once. I had to furnish my wardrobe, and my army pay was scarcely sufficient for so doing. Not having the means to rent a room, and as our barracks were not very tempting—because of the fumes from our African brothers—I hung my hammock betwen two posts of a gallery, and there I spent the nights in the fresh air. " Sleeping in the streets, one offends no one," says Petit-jean. At dawn I would roll up my bed in my overcoat. If, while passing in the streets, I saw a gallery that pleased me more than those I already knew, the following night I would make that one my home. Like a child of the desert, I can laugh at a shelter. The whole globe has become my domicile; I can stop any place I fancy and leave any place I find unpleasant. Did a savage in the forest ever know insomnia! This tirade à la Seneca did not however prevent me from accepting the offer of part of a bed in a house which a friend of mine occupied, and without much urging. I wisely profited by this occasion to sleep well, because as soon as our recruits were sufficiently trained to face the enemy, we entered upon a campaign, and since then I have more often slept on the ground than on a mattress.

I presume that sensible men will not think it a crime that I served under the English flag. Pursued by steel and fire, naked, dying of hunger, I was brought by Fate into an army that was trying to recapture my native land from the Africans who were devastating it. Should I refuse the protection they offered in place of my misery? Should I refuse the occasion to revenge myself upon those barbarous hordes, who were the cause of my ruin and sufferings?

To carry arms against the revolting slaves of Saint Domingue is not to be traitorous to one's country; it is to serve it. It was easy to perceive from the half-hearted efforts of the English that they had no plan to permanently occupy the island after conquering it. Their aim was solely to profit by the resources it offered and to use it as a means of barter after peace was proclaimed. May it please Heaven, for the future good of France, that they succeed in keeping possession of it until that time. If the Negroes succeed in chasing them out, France will only enter another day of loss in torrents of blood.* At the moment these nice islanders give me nearly two hundred *gourdes* a month. For my part, this is what I offer for that sum:

With gun on shoulder and sabre at side,
I show each day my worth and courage
Against the enemy who has persecuted us.
I swim at times through the deep streams;
I climb the mountains and penetrate the forests;
I brave the sun's fierce rays;
At night, upon some straw, I sleep beneath the sky;

* This prophecy was fulfilled in less than a decade, when Napoleon's expeditionary force under General LeClerc reconquered the colony, only to be destroyed itself later.

And with poor food and strong brandy
I appease some of my needs.
To pass the time which often I find boring,
I maneuver my company,
Or rove, when skies are clear,
The surrounding plains,
Both rough and faded,
Which circle our encampments;
I smoke some tobacco, or, at times, make verse;
Think of my present misfortunes,
Of my happy past, and wonder about my unknown future.

At times, however, I find occasion for a few more agreeable pleasures; for example, we are at present in a garrison in Port-au-Prince where they have had us come for rest and recreation after a glorious and fatiguing campaign. Our company takes watch by turns at the different posts which defend the city; and when our service is over we spend the time in a society which is very brilliant.

Port-au-Prince is a big city. The streets are full of elegantly built houses. One finds, as in Cap Français, public squares ornamented with trees and fountains. Happier than the latter city, this one was not as badly burned by Robespierre's cruel Commissioners. The population is large, commerce is very active, and gold and silver are in profusion:

In spite of this, the place has an air
Of a vast camp instead of a city;
Pleasures crowd one another,
But the price of them is high.
The food is of the best,
The wine is of fine vintage,
And one can gamble for large stakes.

144

In the evening there is music
Of splendid quality—for amateurs.
The balls and dances are unique:
One sees grenadiers, infantrymen,
Young faces, old mustaches,
Fans and swords,
Amiable nymphs, and canteen girls,
Petticoats of all kinds,
Hussars of all colors.
It was unfortunate that the festival
Would sometimes end unhappily.
Often to liven the event
Some hot-headed young bloods
Would start a quarrel for this or that.
Among twenty swooning women
They would exchange their sword thrusts,
Their hands propelled by rage.
But more often, as it happened,
During a beautiful caper
The bugle call would sound
And all at once the dancing ceased;
We would know then that the enemy
Was scaling our very walls,
Yet gaily say to our lady fair,
" I will return in just a moment."
But the hunt does not always
Turn out as one hopes,
And some poor devil often went
To Hades to finish out his dance—
If by chance one dances there.

It would be easy to live amicably with our Britannic
comrades. All that is needed is to drink strictly hard
liquor with them each day, and not to contradict when
they repeat to satiety that the English Nation is the
greatest in all the world, in war, commerce, agriculture,

manufacture, customs, sciences, arts, manly strength, womanly charm, social accomplishments, etcetera—and there are countless etceteras. But, unfortunately for the tranquility of the country, there are among us a few who do not admit all of these claims.

The French troops are at least three times as numerous as the English. The latter peacefully guard the posts, and we are sent into active combat. However, there is always care taken to send in an expedition one company of English with several companies of French, in order that they may have the right to give the command to a British officer; and it is this company and this officer who receive the glory of our successes. Never in an official report are the auxiliary companies spoken about. It is always fifty or sixty intrepid English who assaulted and took an enemy post, which actually took the lives of two or three hundred men of our poor regiments.

As war must always involve risk, one side cannot continually be the victor. If the defeat is too evident for the English to deny, the fault is always awarded to the auxiliary troops who failed the invincible ones through faint-heartedness; or else the enemy had an immense superiority in numbers; or some such reason. The fact is that an Englishman cannot be beaten; if you doubt it, you have only to read the history of this extraordinary people, but they can only be well appreciated by living with them and seeing them at close range. This people of many newspapers succeed by means of writing of their virtues, and by believing in them. They would perhaps merit many of their claims if they would not detract from their fine qualities by an insupportable conceit, an atrocious Machiavellism, and that avid love of gold which causes them to sacrifice everything in the world in its

interest. Expressing myself thus, you must know that
I speak of them in general. I also must add:

> One meets from England
> Fine minds and hearts;
> And to a Frenchman, an Englishman can appeal;
> For I have known several
> Whom I love sincerely,
> And whose friendship I hold dear . . .

I believe, my dear sister, that it is time to think of con-
cluding my recital. I started this chapter several months
back and I continued it during the leisure moments I could
find from my duties. I am finishing it during the little
ten-day leave that I am having at Fort Bizoton, where
I have been made a commander.

Between ourselves, it was a boring stay. I am far from
good society and good food, and I sleep only with one
eye closed.

They say that glory is a wonderful thing, for which
one cannot pay too high a price. That may be, but I
wonder.

Book Six

❦

ARGUMENT OF BOOK SIX

My regiment left the high mountains on which it was encamped to go to the aid of the city of St. Marc, surrounded and seized by a large army. We soon lifted the siege and after driving the enemy into the inaccessible gorges which served as their retreat, we took again to the routes of our aerial garrisons. In traversing the beautiful plain of Arcahaye, so prized for the richness of its produce and the hospitality of its inhabitants, my mouth watered; and Major C. de P., who loves pleasure as much as I do, obtained for himself and for me a leave of fifteen days, which we spent (in a country, bacchic, unbelievable, and erotic) with the most agreeable people. Plans of campaign. Review of belligerent parties. Affair of the sapodilla. Siege of the camp, retaken by C. False alarm, river passage, and descent upon an unknown isle. A storm, a surprise, rout and retreat. Last decisive battle, truce, and disbanding of army.

The fame of our exploits carried influence

unto the savage peak of the Mirebalais Moun-
tains, where was perched my friend and com-
rade, Captain C. He engaged me to send the
details of our campaign for the instruction
and encouragement of the young heroes who
wanted to attempt it after us.

Camp Creuzet, Saint Domingue

[APRIL 1796]

FAITHFUL to my promise, my dear comrade, I shall
recount for you that which has occurred to me since the
day when we left you in your palace of clouds to guard
the baggage of our regiment. I will pass lightly over our
military operations, since your neighboring leader has
received full details, but I will expatiate with satisfaction
upon the ways in which the happy inhabitants of Arcahaye
made gracious our sojourn amongst them.

After our separation, we clambered down hill for an
entire night, from the point of the summit where we left
you to the plain which forms its base. Taking only an
hour out, to spend half in sleep, and half in swallowing
a biscuit and cheese, we resumed our route to reach the
main road which followed the coast. Once there, we had
to make twenty miles upon the burning sand between
the sea and the mountain, during the hottest hours of
the day, ever seeing water, yet not having one drop to
drink. Thus we reached the Mont Rouis river, and
though it was under fire from an enemy fort, we rushed
into it headlong. After splashing about like ducks, we
dried ourselves by climbing and assaulting the fort with
bayonets.

We then took the road towards St. Marc, where we
contributed to raising the siege; and for several days we
were occupied in cleaning up the surrounding plains of
the debris left by a previous besieging army. This cam-

paign had nothing in particular to distinguish it from the others. It worked as usual—the enemy routed, comrades killed or wounded, and all manner of privations endured.

Our object accomplished, we retraced our steps and crossed the beautiful countryside of Arcahaye, where the inhabitants had also been experiencing, in their way, much suffering and deprivation. It was here, my dear comrade, that our major and I were inspired to rest, in the bosom of this charming society, from the fatigue and experience we had just come from. Easily obtaining a leave, we made our quarters in the home of our big and fat friend, M. de Z.

You already know that chance had united upon plantations neighboring ours many charming and pretty ladies of the city and country; you further know that our host was shot by Cupid in regard to one of them, and that he expected to offer her his heart and hand. This was, consequently, an excellent occasion to distinguish himself by gallantries; the Major and I lacked neither taste nor imagination, and it was decided that we give a big festival to our neighbors. I wrote (in the name of M. de Z.) the invitation in verse to the ladies, saying the fete would be an evening filled with feasting, music, and dancing. For his part, the Major wrote to all the gentlemen whose talents and presence could contribute to the pleasure of our party; and with the same excusable ruse as used in war, others were invited because of their wealth, hoping they would be stimulated to emulation. The day arrived, the preparations were ready, the sun had set, and the guests assembled.

In the center of the garden were flowers and fruit trees; also, displaying its choicest treasures, was an immense sapodilla, whose long, flexible branches, covered with fruit, touched the grass and made a vast salon of verdure; beneath its foliage the table was set. It appeared to me that I had never beheld a more brilliant scene. Imagine twelve lovely and elegantly dressed women seated at a round table covered with everything luscious—the most deliciously prepared things and fruits of diverse colors and odors filled graceful baskets. The table encircled the tree, which was entwined with garlands and resembled a column of flowers. Lanterns were strung among the branches like fruits of fire, and candles were placed upon the table in enormous bouquets of jasmine that seemed to replace the brilliance of the sun, which had just hid behind the mountains. The sky was serene, only a zephyr moved the leaves, and a murmuring brook could be heard near by. We were refreshed by the wines of France and the fine liqueurs of Italy and Martinique. Champagne soon had its usual effect, and brought gaiety to the table with bright banter and songs of love: I was in my element. Placed between the beautiful Madame d'E. and the seductive Madame N., surrounded by cakes, fruits, and flagons, I had my lyre brought and sang impromptu couplets, interrupted only by a dozen glasses.

After each one had sung in his turn, all arose from the table and the dancing began. At midnight we escorted the ladies home; and at the moment before leaving, M. de T. invited everyone to reunite at his home on the following evening. That being settled, each retired to dream of the pleasures he came from having and of perhaps even sweeter ones to come.

We found at M. de T.'s home the same pleasant people, but a different type of fete. In place of a light supper, it was a splendid dinner, and served in a large and hand-

somely furnished dining room. This formality slightly
retarded our gaiety. Eating was slow, and talk was on
politics, war, and literature; but after awhile, lighter talk
and singing came, as before, with the bottles. I was
named and installed as the Troubadour of the District;
it followed, then, that I must sing one of my songs. But
as I was not as congenially placed as on the previous
evening, the couplets issuing from my head were half sad
and half gay. The gist of them all was this:

> In times past I had much wealth;
> I have not now one sou remaining,
> And for this I feel desolation;
> But the Heavens took not all,
> Since my health, my appetite, my friends are left me,
> And for this, I feel consolation.

After my song, we passed about an hour in reciprocal
consolations; and after that, to change our mood, we gaily
sang and danced as on the night before. A few well-
chosen words of flattery from pretty lips told our friend
Z. that his rustic supper was received with more favorable
approval than this formal dinner. This made him wish
to redouble his desire to please; and after a quarter hour
of consultation with his nearest intimate counsellors, he
invited all the guests to breakfast a few days later in a
charming spot, the whereabouts of which he alone knew—
its only drawback being that it was near enemy territory,
but all present felt rather lightheaded and no attention
was paid to this aspect, and each promised to be prepared
for the exact day and hour.

Already avid Time had devoured four hours of the
appointed day; and Night, the fickle hussy, was preparing
to breakfast with the Antipodes; the Sun, tired of the
caresses of his exacting spouse, was mounting his chariot

to come to our country, to recruit his strength by inhaling the dewy air which Aurora had filled with flowered fragrance. It was five o'clock when, ready from head to foot, we mounted our army steeds to go from plantation to plantation for those who were to be at our breakfast. Our heroines, rendered more careful after reflection, at first refused to go with us; but at last they were convinced that we loved them too much to expose them to useless dangers, so they seated themselves upon their palfreys and followed bravely their gallant cavaliers. We had gone already two and a half miles at a gallop, and in order to give our horses time to rest, we stopped at the edge of a wood, discoursing on the pleasures of a good breakfast after exercise. All at once, we saw running towards us a Negro, panting and frightened. He announced that a horde of brigands were devouring our near-by repast. At this terrible intelligence we saw anger, fear, and hunger spread among us—one growing red, another pale, and another pulling a long face, each according to his dominant emotion. We assembled, remained close together, and prepared arms; the men wanted to defend their breakfast at sword point; the women wanted to retreat. Glory, Fright, and Hunger held a long discussion, but at last the fair sex carried the day.

We turned back in disappointment and reproached one another for our misadventure. M. d'E., especially, was furious to have been made to arise so early for nothing. One said he was dying of thirst; another complained of an empty stomach; and someone else claimed to have a headache. Added to this was the fact that the nearest plantation was nearly three miles away, and that the hour for breakfast was past. Certainly the situation was deplorable! I do not remember what pretext we used in saying we had to leave the main road to take a cross-country one, but we had them descend a steep ravine surrounded by log-wood trees. We led the way and pushed aside some branches—O Heaven, what a scene! In the center of the ravine, where ran a limpid brook, was a little island, shaded from the sun by an impenetrable grove. There, upon the grass, sat a large, cold pâté de foie gras, its vast circumference attesting to the number of goose livers that went into its making, resting upon a cushion of mushrooms. Further on was an enormous turkey, hardly able to hold the truffles with which it was filled. There was a glazed ham, a stuffed tongue, salads, and creams. Everywhere to be seen were flowers, fruits, and bottles only waiting to be opened. What a moving spectacle for famished travellers who had believed they would not breakfast at all!

Each one grasped a mat of straw to use as a chair; a banana leaf served as a plate. Reclining like Turks did not cause us to eat with less appetite, and soon all that could be seen about us were turkey bones, fruit seeds, and empty bottles.

As our first festival had inspired other hosts, this one piqued the honor and ambition of another of our neighbors; and the day was set for a reunion at the plantation of M. de B. For this one, the weather was beautiful; only a few light clouds at times lessened the heat of the sun. All the convivial company was ready with gaiety and good appetite. M. de B. had placed the splendid dinner beneath a tall and thick trellis of Muscat grapes, worthy of those of Canaout, and these were interlaced with golden passion-flowers, which bent their branches within reach. At the four corners of the trellis, flowering orange trees gave forth a delicate fragrance, which mingled well with that of the cooking fricassees.

The heavens, it seemed, tried to add to our pleasure, and we sat down to dine favored by the most perfect weather imaginable. The main course of our dinner had yielded to our attack, and each according to his taste was savoring the tender pink skin of the sapodilla, the cream of the *cavernitte*, the soft almond flavor of the avocado, or the sweet acid of the pineapple.

All at once the sky became covered with heavy black clouds. A gale of wind extinguished the candles, which had not long been lighted, and left us only the light that came in rapid flashes from the heavens. Rolls of thunder, which at first came from a distance, rapidly approached and burst with terrific claps, which multiplied in echoes through the near-by mountains, at last rending the clouds and letting fall upon us tons of rain.

We rose in tumult—the table was knocked over; the platters, dishes, glasses, cakes, fruits, creams, all floated pell-mell; the ladies made umbrellas of their skirts; and each escaped as best he could. In this uproar I was per-haps the only one who retained some calm. I covered my head with a large salad bowl, put in each pocket a bottle of champagne, and seizing in each arm the two prettiest ladies of the party, hastened to the house, which was about a hundred feet from the trellis. All the fugitives were hurrying there, and soon we were busy trying to get dry. During this occupation M. de B. was preparing his expression of condolences to us all; that is to say, he added with much taste an elegant collation, which well recompensed us for the bath and the exercise we took before ending our dinner.

However, the weather redoubled its efforts, and we

braved all, at our ease, and passed part of the night in
drinking and singing, bothering little how much rain fell,
or how strong the wind blew. As for me, between two
bottles and between two pretty women, I made love at
right and at left. Pleasantries escaped my lips by the
dozen, I recounted funny stories, and when it came my
turn to sing, I summoned a few couplets, and everyone
joined in the chorus.

Happily, the wine never ceased to flow until the rain
ceased to fall, and then each retired to his home in mud
to his knees and wine to his eyes. Alas! Upon my return
I found something that sobered me. It was an order to
rejoin the army. But, as we were invited to spend the
following evening at the plantation of M. d'E., I waited
to depart the day following this last festivity. This one
was as enjoyable as the others that preceded. I have no
time to give the dinner menu; but join a good middle-class
cook to a perfect chef, add prized recipes from the best
books, find the finest dishes, the most elegant desserts,
the wines of greatest savor, and you will have an idea
of our repast. But the Ports! One would need have been
there to appreciate them. They well realized from my
devouring appetite and my insatiable thirst, that it was
the last time that I would be in their good company. A
little incident, which at first seemed to dampen the general
gaiety, turned out on the contrary to add to our amusement.

In opening a bottle of champagne I pointed it toward
the prettiest lady in the circle, who was hit on the forehead by the cork and gave forth a cry of pain. When we
found she was more frightened than hurt, the group surrounded me and proposed to conduct a court-martial, and
after a very learned discussion, I was led to the knees of
the wounded to receive the punishment which she felt

suited the crime. " I am at your command," I told her; " decide my fate. I will accept it without complaint. I am even ready, if I must, to empty the bottle that I so awkwardly uncorked." " No, no," responded my gracious judge. " You must have a punishment that profits everyone. I condemn you to put into verse the compliments and excuses you have made to me." I had to submit; I coughed, I blew my nose, I scratched my head; then, taking the tone and manner of a dispirited lover and emitting an anguished sigh, I hurriedly wrote:

> Since an almost fatal blow outraged
> The perfection of your lily brow
> I have trembled in turn with pain and fear;
> And if it were possible to show my heart,
> You would see the wound that is imprinted there!

About midnight everyone prepared to leave. How painful was this moment for me! I could not help realizing the difference between the life I had just been living and the one that awaited me at camp. In song I made my farewells to our little society:

> Alas! Tomorrow I shall take my leave
> From all the things for which I care.
> Here you know so well how to unite
> Love with Bacchus and with Wisdom.
> Gay friends and charming ladies,
> Of you I shall unceasingly dream;
> Would that I might take with me your parting words
> To replace my heart, which I do leave with you.

That cursed morrow arrived—but I will not trouble you in recounting the feelings I had; you would mock at my weakness. It would indeed be a hard and savage heart that could abandon, without regret, these happy surroundings, blessed by Nature, and where every day one could see, hear, and admire the attractive Mme. d'E., her pretty sister, her interesting nieces, the beautiful Mme. B., the good Mme. de M., and her charming husband, the Colonel, our host. Here, my dear comrade, is how I passed my leave, in the center of a thousand varied pleasures; while you are perched upon the high peaks of the Mirebalais Mountains, sleeping on a plank, lodged under a piece of cloth; where your days are varied by military duties, salt meat, bad bread or yams baptized in rum—not to mention grouching Creoles.

Book Seven

⚜

ARGUMENT OF BOOK SEVEN

I was placed in command of a post perched upon the summit of a mountain which separated the part of the island which was intact from the part which had been ravaged by the insurrection. I profited from this position by taking poetic walks on one side and then on the other, and I paint my country in the double perspective which was offered by these views. Exordium and Invocation. Scene of the mountains under cultivation of coffee, cocoa, etc. The episode of Anacoana. Glimpse of the peaceful plains with their crops of sugar and tobacco. Picture of massacre and conflagration. Address to philosophers. Conclusion.

Camp Bizoton, Saint Domingue
[JUNE 1797]

From these impenetrable ramparts
Where the God of War has assembled his children,
This place since ages past
Has opposed combat with its crushing sorrows.
Ah! Let me but flee for a day War's tasks and duties,
And, far from a coarse multitude
Will I wander at leisure in my solitary walks
Through these valleys so loved by Heaven.
Soon, if my desire can sustain my courage,
Will I climb the far off Mornes, and reach the untamed crest
Which separates a peaceful, natural garden
From a desert camp, defiled by carnage.
There will I scan with hungry eyes
The places where I stray
And picture these two countrysides.
Since I have shed my burdensome armor,
I have left wild Mars behind for gentle Nature,
And by my irksome duties I no longer am tormented.
All about me seems embellished to give me pleasure;
I now can breathe with freedom and release.
My hurrying feet seem hardly even to touch the earth.
I feel like a young canary which from his cage has fled,
Warbling his happiness and flying to adventure;
Tasting the grain just caught in passing,
And at the edge of the murmuring brook,
Drinking with delight the water purely running.
As I go along this narrow path,
Lemon blossoms perfume my passage!
Farther on I perceive the elegant bitter-almond trees
Whose extending arms form spreading arches,

163

And beneath the shade of their heavy foliage
I shall, if I can, forget myself
And only enjoy the present. The sweet ambrosia
Of the pineapple, for which thirst has increased my ardor,
The orange blossoms, just opening,
Exhale about me their most tender fragrance.
That miniature and butterfly-like creature,
The hummingbird, painted with rainbow hues,
Is almost hidden in a single flower while sipping dew,
And balancing itself upon its airy wings,
Brings me solace while I watch it,
And recalls to me my childhood.
Let others go into the silent woods;
Their aspect saddens too much my soul.
Here, all speaks to my ears and eyes—
The timid songster softly practices his scales,
The parakeet tries out his words,
The wood-pecker knocks upon the bark.
The very trees, hardly ever silent,
Echo their own sweet special music.
One cries at each breeze that passes,
Another whistles out its melody
Among the long straight branches.
I recognize the cinnamon by the rustling of its foliage;
The ebony tree overhead shakes its tiny bells.
All about, I admire the treasures
That Nature has lavished on our fecund isle.
The young mocha plants, transplanted to our shores,
Have become the pride of the whole new world.
Today, all red with seeds, the full-ripe mocha
Calls for the busy hands of the tardy reaper;
The signal is given, and everything begins to stir.
The Negroes enjoy themselves by singing as they work;
Some go to pick the vermillion coffee berries,
So hard and glossy upon the slopes;

Others go to empty the loaded baskets;
This harvest dries beneath the heat of day.
Next, emptied in the pit of the circular cutter,
The grindstone smashes the bean's light shell,
And the rapid sifter in its turn
Separates the grain from the useless husk.
O precious coffee, gracious liquid,
You awaken my mind and sustain my courage;
Bacchus' fruits take precedence in sweetness,
But with them you receive my homage.
The massive oak, the lofty pine
Stand out in their strange elegance,
As do the papaya and the cocoanut palm;
And I salute you, O banana tree,
Whose golden bunches almost touch the ground.
The Negro picks them as his bread, and, thanks to kind Nature,
Each day, without effort, finds in them a portion of his food.
Here, the arts come to search
From among the log-wood a necessary dye;
There, from the leaves of the Napal Fig
Comes an emblem of royalty, as this humble fruit tree
Furnishes a brilliant purple.
Further on, the nutritious coconut abounds
And under its thick coating tries to hide.
I love to see this path, so gently turning,
And tracing itself upon the side
Of our mountains, steep and verdure-clad.
Far off, and walking in perfect file,
Are innumerable mules carrying their loads,
While from here they seem as if suspended in the air;
They are transporting to the city
The gifts of our clime, to cross the ocean
For the needs of twenty different peoples.
Whilst abandoning myself to this rustic scene,
Time is fleeting, and a day so precious to me

165

Is half gone by.
The midday sun beats fiercely down
As when the ancient islanders of yore
Loved it as a god and cherished it as a father.
But I must find a denser shade
Against its burning rays—
Here, beneath this huge and cursèd fig tree,
Whose great branches form an impenetrable front,
The happy Indians once gathered.
What lamentable memories
Must this giant tree possess!
Ancient Xaraga, tragic and famous plain,
I wish to place a flower upon your last queen's tomb.
Daughter of the Sun, honorable and kind
Anacoana * reigned over an innocent people,
Whose days were passed in peace. What unknown race,
They asked, was it who came across the big deep water?
These were White men. The wondering natives
Saw them come, equipped with fire, descending
From a wingèd monster.
Though their lips were smiling, an evil genius
From under a veil of friendship hid their traitorous hearts.
Beneath this cursèd fig tree was the accustomed place
Of the chieftain's councils and their native games.
Here, confident and disarmed, they assembled
To admire and feast the strangers.
The queen made haste to offer what treasures
Could be gathered for the visitors she wished to welcome.
Ovando,† however, saw with a furtive glance much wealth,

* Anacoana, wife of Caonabo, Indian Cacique at the time Columbus discovered Santo Domingo in 1492, was killed by Ovando, the Spanish Governor.

† Nicolas de Ovando, b. Valodolid, 1460, d. Madrid, 1518. This Spanish Administrator arrived in Santo Domingo in 1502 with 30 vessels and 2,500 men. Under him the Indians were virtually

Along with this people's candor and their gifts.
He came for pillage; their golden ornaments
Spoke loud of what he wanted.
Smiling with anticipation, he made ready the crime.
"Queen," he said, "we will now prepare for you a festival;
The pretended assaults of our prudent soldiers
Will amuse and instruct you in the art of combat."
Having spoken, soon the perfidious phalanx
Around the august tree in battle form arrayed;
The signal sounded. O pinnacle of baseness!
For the simulated games these credulous spectators
Awaited—only to receive cold steel or bullets of hot lead,
And fall wounded or dead like timid sheep!
Anacoana—upon you, without feeling for your rank,
Your gentle sex, your friendliness,
These tigers used a tree—a fatal rope . . .
Alas! My Muse, in tears, can say no more!
O plains of Haiti, O unfortunate country,
To eternal suffering are you thus condemned!
Yet what other view superb! What varied aspect!
I now can see assembled at my feet
The richest gifts that the earth can offer.
I can see all about me now
Busy workers, great houses with their cabins,
The flowering plains and the vast fields of cane,
And the Blacks working in rows, singing
And lifting their hoes in even cadence;
The cattle soon will gather to their sheds
By smooth and shaded roads
That cut in squares the fertile plains.
The heavy wagons fully laden
Are driven by well-trained hands,
And however hard it is to turn the wheels,

exterminated and African slaves extensively introduced to replace
them. Diego Colón, Columbus' son, superseded him in 1509.

And the mighty oxen and the mules move on.
But another picture comes to afflict my eyes!
I can clearly see the den of crimes,
The results of great disaster and of suffering,
And the tombs of many victims.
Alas, these burnt plains serve but to remind me
Of that first time, how as a pupil of Bellona
I avenged my friends, so vilely slain;
These memories, to this day, shake me to my very soul.
O day, unequaled in my memory,
O frightful day, which by flame and steel
Saw the dead strewn thick and made a Hell,
This island, once the rival of Elysium!
That fatal moment, when a favorite slave
Became the first headsman to betray his master . . .
God! I shudder still; an adored wife
Beheld a cherished husband stabbed,
And near his bleeding body
Was delivered to horrible indignities.
Hapless one! She died, and her last look
Blessed the charitable blade
That ended her sorrow, shame, and suffering!
Another victim also in their power,
With graying hair and bewildered eyes,
Was beseeching mercy;
Her dying cries mingled with those
Of her son's young children,
Whose bodies were cast upon their mother's expiring form!
Other Whites, escaping the first furies,
Hid in darkened archways,
Thinking there to find a haven—
A vain, deluded hope.
Already the conflagration was ignited;
It spread; and soon in its cruel course
It reached and embraced all things.

Beneath its irresistible rage
Marble became ashes and steel dissolved.
The fire, divided into tongues of flame,
Escaped and appeared from a hundred different roads;
Then again reunited in one immense brazier
Which at that moment seemed to rival the sun;
Burning particles blew through the air;
All the fields in the distance were covered with cinders
And the smoke, winding in enormous clouds,
Made fantastic designs in the sky.
All was over, and the parched walls, without support,
Collapsed with a terrific din.
Deprived of more combustibles,
The fire, in a last mighty effort,
Revived and leaped in painted columns.
One would think, in its rage, it wished to burn the sky;
But it drooped, languished, and died exhaling
A trail of black and spiraling smoke
Which the winds did blow about.
You murderers, who only lately were barbarians,
This fatal spot will be your destiny.
Unfortunates! No doubt in your long orgy,
When more conflict will consume your land,
You will regret the steel which disrupted your quiet life!
And you, my comrade, like me saved only by hazard
From some horrible butchery or perfidious sword,
And O my companions in misery,
Was this escape fortunate or no?
Condemned to a vile estate
Must we go from place to place,
Dragging out our broken existence,
Or else turn soldier,
To become the prey of scoundrels
While avenging this disastrous crime?
Here then is this country, whose possession

169

Excited jealousy in the stranger's breast.
Alas! It offers now to my pitying heart
Only a picture of endless desolation.
You it is who caused this fearful suffering,
Vain and ignorant Philosophers,
With Humanity upon your lips
But never within your wicked hearts!
Feigning to believe the tales
Of romantic impostors who painted our island
From cold attics in their distant city!
You pretend to pity the unhappiness
Of the care-free Negro, who is protected in youth,
Nursed in sickness, and retired in old age;
While from the bosom of luxury and idleness,
You repulse with indignities
The suffering victims who tell you of the misery
Of white men, of Frenchmen, of your brothers!
See now the slave—free but miserable,
Polluted by the blackest crimes,
Cursing your questionable benefits
Which have rendered him wretched and unhappy . . .
But already the God of Day
Approaches quickly in his chariot
And reminds me to hasten my return;
Already the impatient drum
Recalls me to new dangers.
My Muse, in vain, wants me to stay;
But austere Duty must not cede to Pleasure,
And so I leave my lute to retake my arms.

Book Eight

❦

ARGUMENT OF BOOK EIGHT

The English, seeing that their projects on Saint Domingue were costing them too much money and too many soldiers, took the means to evacuate. They were ordered to leave our six thousand auxiliary Africans, well trained and well armed, to render one day the conquest of the country more difficult for the new French Government; and after donating to the White officers six months' pay, they had them transported to the American continent. My family was in New York; I joined them in that city. Soon after my arrival, my Colonel, who had settled in the environs of Philadelphia, induced me to spend a delightful vacation at his place. I start my trip. Since my mother had made me promise to recount to her all the incidents of this little voyage, I write from each place where I spend a few days.

I MISLED you when I implied I would not have to leave until after breakfast. My intention was then to prevent bidding you good-bye, which perhaps would make me renounce a trip which I honestly did not want to miss. What regrets I have in leaving you must cede to the repeated invitations of that good and generous man who was for a long time my chief and always my friend.

Since I am absenting myself from the best of mothers, I will try to ease her pain by frequent letters, showing her how much she is in my thoughts. My first one, no doubt, will be from Elizabethton, where I expect to remain a week. My intention is to stop in this way for a few days in the cities and villages along my route, where I find friends. I will write you whenever possible, and since your maternal partiality makes you enjoy my verses, I will pray my Muse to double her laziness and please you with a few lines. But I hope that you will not notice that in writing them I am on the run, and upon an entirely different mount than Pegasus.

Upon awakening, you will find a note upon your dressing table. I left upon it a thousand kisses of good-bye, asking your forgiveness in making my furtive leave:

> You well know that happy by your side
> I would always like to be;
> And I wish each day by the gentlest of acts
> To assure you of my tenderest affection.
> But friendship calls, and your loving heart

173

Knows too well that noble emotion
Not to speed me on my way.
Good-bye! I leave you now with tears.
You will also cry, but I am sure
That while yet sighing, your unselfish lips
Will be wishing me a Bon Voyage . . .

Aboard the Packet

The mother and brother of Madame de P. whom you know, are most agreeable traveling companions. They decided to go to Elizabethton by water, which suited me well. I have made the trip several times by land, but did not yet know this way, which seems less fatiguing and more agreeable, thanks to the varied perspectives which the passing banks ceaselessly offer.

Faithful to the promise I made you, I am writing you a letter which, no doubt, you will have much trouble in deciphering, but I have an excuse. A coil of rope is my chair, a beer barrel, my desk. The passengers cast long whirls of tobacco smoke in my eyes. If I were more at ease, I would paint for you the beautiful view which the New York harbor offers. But, in rising to look for a more favorable place to write, I left the fundamental portion of my pants on some tar which had been spilled upon my " chair ":

Decency demands I remain sitting down
Upon the throne which I still must use,
For fear that the light breezes
My coat-tails may lift,
And so offer to some profane glances
What should only be shown one's apothecary . . .

However, I can see from here the elegant houses which border the Battery—its large promenade, which by its advantages can become the most beautiful in the world when the Americans have formed their taste and become less tenacious with their money—I can also see the small office building where the merchants, armed with binoculars, go each day at high tide to await the arriving ships. I can distinguish the different meeting places of the newspaper reporters.

There, too, are found the Federalists, who, while desiring to send our French soldiers by the twenties of thousands, become impatient because the results are not quick enough. The Republicans also gather here—who go about expressing wishes for our success, and do not call us " French Dogs." Is this for love of us, or only in the spirit of contradiction?

In truth, we are generally seen with a jaundiced eye, which does not surprise me. All things concerning us arrive in America through English lantern slides, which do not flatter their objects. And we are too indifferent to consider defending ourselves. Our implacable and eternal enemy, who is both clever and ungenerous, neglects nothing that will serve to do us harm. Little or big, vile or noble, any means is good to him, and for this the press is used to the best advantage. Slanderous and defamatory pamphlets are sent in profusion to the four corners of the globe to be distributed gratis, or sold dirt-cheap, to historians, poets, novelists, philosophers, reporters, etc. Writers vie for the honor of painting us in the most hideous and ridiculous colors. Even school books are marred by caricatures designed to inculcate in young minds unjust antipathy, which England believes to her interest to create and nourish against a rival nation. Americans—who have not till the present any literature but that of the mother country—have naturally gathered from childhood false ideas about us, which, no doubt, their good sense will later rectify.

I can no longer see the Battery. At my right, the green and cultivated river-bank extends farther on to form the East River; at my left, the Hudson River carries majestically to the sea her immense tributary waters. Upon both sides rise innumerable masts which seem to rise from the cities and mix with the church steeples, and there are as many here as in a European city. All these objects appear and pass and reappear again. Now I see ships passing in full sail to the Narrows which is formed by Long and Staten Islands. It seems that Nature has expressly placed these two islands so that New York can have the largest, safest, and most convenient port. We are now entering the arm of the sea which separates the hilly part of the island from the flat part of New Jersey; and I appear to be sailing on one of those peaceful rivers, which, in its twisting course, fertilizes the productive country side.

Elizabethton—July

Upon disembarking, Col. C., the innkeeper, brought us some punch, and had the stage coach summoned to take us to the city, which was a few miles from the river. This honest Republican is not the only one in this country where the new Cincinnatus has left the field of glory for more humble stations. In Philadelphia, Col. S. makes shoes; in Baltimore, Major R. took my measurements for a suit; and all the farms are peopled with generals, colonels, and captains. On the other hand, one sees many individuals who were formerly shoemakers, tailors, or bricklayers, now rich and with a place in society. Here more than anywhere else one finds the theatre of games of chance.

The stage deposited us in front of M. T. de la T.'s house, where my traveling companions were expected. Since then each day has brought a new party. The most brilliant was the house-warming of M. de M., a rich man of Martinique, established three miles from Elizabethton. All the distinguished inhabitants were invited, which made carriages very scarce. I could find only a variety of cabriolet, which had been repaired with tops of wine boxes. I ventured in the ambulating wine cask, hoping that the descending curtain of night would hide me from laughter. Vain hope! I was seen by a dozen pranksters. One asked me for the price of a beer; others wanted a drink of claret. One told me it would be better for me to carry the carriage, instead of exposing myself to being carried in it. Another said I should have put a candle in the stomach of my poor skinny horse in order to have it serve as a lantern. He was trotting a little faster, when, in a fatal moment, my brave steed was frightened by a piece of flying paper and began to fly, it seemed, dragging his fractured carriage. Soon we found ourselves in a ditch in ten pieces. The animal, stretched upon the ground, soon became quiet and started to amuse himself by reaching out his tongue to get some pieces of nearby hay. A farm house was close to this scene of action. Here I requested a stall for Rozinante, a comb and brush for myself, and after repairing the disorder of my clothes, I finished my journey on foot.

The ball commenced soon after my arrival. Dancing was in the large hallway, and the rooms opening upon it on either side contained all types of games of chance. Every minute servants could be seen passing from one room to the other with refreshments and liqueurs of all varieties. At midnight double doors were opened and one could see a large semi-circular table, profusely covered with all that America and Europe could offer to the service of Comus.

The table was surrounded with ladies, and I must here render justice to the truth: they ate more than was becoming to the fair sex and made us suffer pangs of hunger for nearly an hour. Unable to contain myself further, I said to them in a voice almost inaudible with weakness:

> Being near you young beauties
> Fills our eyes and hearts,
> But we must say, by your leave,
> That our stomachs are aggrieved;
> Forgive us!

This eloquent harangue caused them to beat a hasty retreat, and soon taking the places they vacated, we made a ferocious attack upon the supply which they spared us. We would not have left a vestige, but a mission composed of the prettiest young ladies came to propose an armistice. Too gallant to refuse, we set forth upon a hundred dance figures, only putting ourselves in better condition to continue our feasting. At three o'clock in the morning onion soup was served; at five, tea or coffee; at eight, breakfast. After this last repast everyone refreshed himself with several hours of sleep, then returned to finish the day by playing different kinds of games. However, this afternoon, at four, I am going to leave this agreeable company. But since I was able to leave you, I shall bear without complaint all other departures.

Trenton—July

We left on the 25th the happy town of Elizabethton. The cold was excessive and the North wind cut the face; the preceding day, however, was overwhelmingly warm. This variation in temperature undoubtedly contributes to the maladies of the lungs which ravage this part of the country. Another cause is the constant use of salted provisions which render the blood acid, hot, and thick. I really believe that uncleanliness also adds something by engendering skin diseases, which have their repercussions in the number of charlatans that swarm America.

> Each morning in a bowl of water,
> Milady dips her face
> Even to her neck, but further—no;
> She also scrubs her hands
> Even to the elbow, but further—no;
> For custom or modesty forbids!

In contrast, they put much stock in cleanliness that shows. They put a mirror-finish on their furniture; the floors are washed almost each day; their outer clothing is glistening white. One must remember that day by day all is changing for the better. The number of foreigners who are coming to establish themselves in the United States are introducing the manners and customs of Europe. Already public baths are being established in the big cities; the custom of blowing one's nose in the fingers has ceded to that of using a pocket handkerchief; people are beginning to have their teeth attended to by dentists; and they now actually believe that it is not polite to belch in public in such a way that causes the house to shake.

179

This country is certainly not the same as when I arrived for the first time, and it is natural to believe that in a few more years it will not be as it is today.

Scarcely had each of us placed ourselves between two thin or plump haunches, which squeezed us all the way to Trenton, than the sky became covered with clouds, and soon a pouring rain forced us to unroll the leather curtains of our stage. They pretended to shelter us, but only succeeded in preventing us from seeing the countryside. Thus seated on benches cushioned with sawdust, jostled to and fro by continual shaking, wet, spattered, and poisoned by the exhalations of a dozen persons vigorously jolted after eating, I finally arrived at the home of friends who were awaiting me.

M. R., heretofore a rich merchant of St. Marc, lives on the revenue of a garden he cultivates a mile from Trenton. Such is the condition of nearly all the refugees of Saint Domingue.

> Raised in ease amidst pleasant surroundings,
> Accustomed to having most wishes fulfilled,
> Now in a dark abyss of misery,
> Destiny with one stroke hurled them down,
> And heaped them with suffering in a strange land,
> Where chance had suddenly brought them—
> Yet, one sees them meet without fear
> Both hard work and privation;
> One sees them bear without wail
> The cares of exile and the scars of want.

One is a gardener, another a school teacher; this one makes marionettes, that one gives concerts; some teach dancing, others sell confections; the shrewdest ones go into business, and some have already become well enough known to be considered illustrious personages. For you know that here gold is the first title of nobility.

And I, after my savings from the army are at an end—to what occupation will I devote myself? Upon thinking it over in the best way I can, and especially remembering the advice and offers of our good neighbor, the Doctor L., I can only see the profession of apothecary, which accords with the one I performed before. Attacking people with little bullets of lead or with little bullets of mercury kills them just the same; it is only the quality in the metal that differs. And perhaps I will reproach myself less for murdering them with balls than with pills. M. R., more pacific, plants, as I have said, carrots and cabbages. His wife is an excellent lady and also attends to the garden; in fact, in conjunction with her husband, she grows and cultivates with care the prettiest little garden I ever saw.

Trenton, the capital of Jersey, is famous for a defeat of part of the English army and for the wise manoeuvers that were made by General Washington. The city is composed of three little sections separated by fields, but it will soon, no doubt, become one. It is advantageously situated on the Delaware, which is crossed by means of a ferryboat; there is talk of building a superb port of modern construction.

A number of French have located in the city and its environs. Those which I have visited did all in their power to render my stay agreeable, and I thanked them most sincerely. They wished to detain me, but:

> Tomorrow I leave for other places
> Where friendship guides.
> But when shall I see again that spot
> Where resides, for me, my happiness!
> Here, I am among pleasures;

I enjoy good wine and good food;
I see men making merry
And women made to please;
Yet midst these amusements
My heart sighs alone;
Nothing is worth more than the sweet leisure
That I share with my mother.

Bristol—July

The first stage that left this morning had but one vacant seat which I took; and Madame de M. waited with her son for a carriage which would pass two hours later. I was sorry about this disappointment, but, after all, the bad is never without some mixture of good. I was badly shaken up that day upon the rugged road. When the rain fell in torrents, I had agreeable conversation with my fellow traveling companions:

Today, by contrast,
I had for neighbors three Negresses,
And two " country-girls " who would have
Pleased me more had they been silent;
But it was the loveliest of mornings,
And never was the air more pure.
Faithful lover of Nature that I am,
I admired her gracious benefits
And forgot the road, the carriage, and those therein.

It was eight o'clock before I arrived in Bristol. I saw at the door of the tavern a man who weighed at least 500 pounds. I thought he was a life-like sign, and I went in for lunch. The first course which was served was a newspaper, this being the usual beginning. From President to chimney-sweep, everyone in America reads half a dozen morning newspapers and perhaps as many in the evening. Some are Republican, others are Federalist, and they insult each other mutually. I was at the table with a gentleman of this latter party. He began the conversation with a critical account of France and her inhabitants, such as one finds in Smollett, Goldsmith, etc., etc. I replied to him as well as I could, and this was exciting him a bit when my host of the 500 pounds entered the room and came to sit down with us. He was an ardent Republican; so, as the Federalist was attacking me, he took up my cause and vented his private opinion on the subject of this discussion. " By God," he said, knocking the table with his fists and causing all the plates to dance.

> By his voice, his gesture, and his air,
> But chiefly by his knuckles,
> I now felt that France was in the hands of Competence;
> Then I departed without ceremony,
> Leaving my men to speak at ease
> Of a country which, parenthetically,
> They only knew by name.

I had eaten in the fashion of the country, meaning that I had amalgamated in my stomach a dozen gelatinous biscuit of medieval origin impregnated with butter, a quarter of a pound of smoked beef cut in slices as thin as paper, six fresh eggs emptied into a tumbler and seasoned with salt, pepper, and mustard, together with a few slices of bread and a plate of cucumber salad—all swimming in an enclosure in which there was at least a pint of watery coffee. To digest this appalling conglomeration with the proper and congenial chemicals, I walked over all this town. Like those of its size, it consists of a long and wide street cut by many cart-wheels, with pretty brick houses scattered among the simple cottages, giving it a rustic appearance, mingled with the glamorous paraphernalia of the city dwellings.

I saw the militia of the district under arms. The officers were in full uniforms of blue and red, with large gilded sabres, shining epaulettes, and a round hat mounted with a high plume. The soldiers wore uniforms of their multifarious trades; each carried his gun as he chose and marched in his own style. I often had occasion to hear or to read their few compliments to us, for other things as well as for our military art; and upon these there always follows mockery of the national vanity of France.

Bristol is, like Trenton, situated on the Delaware. Upon the arrival of Madame de M. we will set out to cross the river to get to Burlington, which is exactly opposite. Impatient to get to the other side, and to shorten the time, I am enjoying myself by writing to you.

> When the time does come to return to you,
> May my good fortune prevent
> Any obstacle from arising
> To detain me upon this bank;
> But if, despite my hopes, Fate does
> Try to delay my leaving,
> My heart will go to that shore
> Where you are and give me
> Courage to take my leave.

Burlington—July

In this country, the little town of Burlington is one in which I would like to live, as much for its picturesque location as for the society that one finds here. Leaving the ferry, I went right to the house of Madame d'E., who is as good and as beautiful as she was in Arcahaye. She met me, as she is accustomed to receiving those whom she esteems, and I had again one of those dinners which her cook prepares so well, and which Madame d'E.'s charm makes so agreeable. After the repast, we amused ourselves by going through the prettiest sections of the town.

> Greenbank is in truth
> One of the loveliest of promenades;
> Twenty elegant facades
> Artfully decorate one side,
> And, upon the other, shade trees
> Caress with bashful kiss
> The grass, brilliant with flowers.
> The catalpas with white clusters,
> The poplars with long branches,
> The willows, emblems of tears,
> Offer everywhere a cooling shade;
> Which, however, allows the eye
> To see the gracious haunts
> Which adorn the opposite shore.

Toward evening a friend suggested taking me to the house of some rich Americans who had invited him to a formal tea. We would enjoy ourselves greatly, he told me, and would meet the most important people in town. So we went along.

Seven o'clock rang when we entered a spacious room, ornate with pictures of English victories and covered with a fine woolen carpet, the very sight of which, due to the season, bathed me in perspiration.

There, twenty persons of the two sexes, dressed as for a wedding, were seated in a half circle, immobile as figures in the wax museum. Feeling like the victim who is dragged to the altar, I crossed the space which separated me from the mistress of the house. I stopped short and made a profound bow, while my guide held my hand and said: " Madame, here is my friend, Mr. P." The lady with a nod of the head said, " How are you, Sir? " I, with another bow, said, " Very well Madame, I thank you." This was only half of my exercises for the evening. The most troublesome remained to come, and it was necessary for me to execute this with good grace. My friend frequently demanded of me to half-circle to the right. Often without leaving me time to rest, it was necessary for me to retrace the steps which I had made, in order to be introduced to each gentleman according to the correct usage and custom; and each of these gentlemen, so as to show me his friendliness, shook my hand until the tears began to come into my eyes. My wanderings ended, I accepted with pleasure the chair which was offered me and shared for a half hour the serious immobility of my neighbors, masculine and feminine. However, as a desire to yawn took me by surprise, I turned my head toward the window and the mistress of the house, persuaded that it was in order to look into the street, said to me politely, " The weather is very beautiful, Sir." That was the beginning of our conversation, and I replied, " Very fine, Madame." Here there was a little pause of several minutes, when one of my neighbors interrupted and asked me if there would not be rain during the night. To this I responded with great wisdom that I really did not know.

After this interesting dialogue, a servant came in and placed in the center of the parlor a round mahogany table, brilliantly polished. Soon the table disappeared beneath a large Chinese tray containing a teapot, sugar bowl, and milk pitcher of silver, surrounded by a dozen cups and saucers of pretty porcelain. Then began the triumph of the mistress of the house. She sat before the table, grave as a judge in session, filling the cups and having them passed around, rinsing them in a bowl of hot water, which was brought, and sending them forth again—and all with an air of importance and ceremony that was extraordinary. During the operation her eyes looked over her guests in order to guess their needs, and she directed in an undertone her butlers, who passed the cakes and confections.

Woe betide the stranger, ignorant or timid! He is not shown pity. They would have him swill tea to his uvula. As for me, more fortunate than wise, I had not emptied my cup by the fourth round, so I evaded the question of replenishment. After the table was removed the conversation became a little more animated. " You came from New York, Monsieur? " " Yes, Madame." " Have you as pretty towns in France? " " We have some of all kinds, Monsieur." " Is it true that Frenchmen live only on vegetables, soup, and frogs? " " I read that this was said of us by several English authors, Madame." " It is strange, Monsieur, that you are as tall and healthy as an American." " Men are alike in all countries, Miss." " And women, Monsieur? " " There are pretty ones everywhere." " Are not the French most interested in frivolity? " " Just as much are they interested in serious things, Madame; their mind is a flexible one, and they know how to judge the time, place and circumstances, and the character of the people with whom they find themselves."

The conversation ceased upon this subject for a few minutes, awakened a little upon talk about politics, and finished by sleeping again upon the rain and fair weather. I left them to sleep at their leisure, and I went to do so

in my bed. An English tea is certainly an important ceremony, but I prefer our good and gay suppers.

Juliet's Cradle—August

Forgive me for remaining so long without writing you,
but we have at the Colonel's such a large group of guests,
and our time has been so well planned with parties and
pleasures, that it has been impossible for me to find enough
quiet for a writer who wishes to be well understood.

"Juliet's Cradle," the country house of Monsieur de
P., is four miles from Burlington on the river and de-
lightfully situated. The Colonel so named it, for hardly
had he taken possession than his wife presented him next
day with a pretty baby girl, whom they named Juliette.
I found all the family doing well, happy and satisfied.

> When, covered with blood and dust,
> My Colonel guided his regiment
> In his brilliant and dangerous career
> He acquitted himself most nobly;
> When receiving honors
> For his glorious deeds,
> He no doubt shone much brighter,
> But he was much less happy.

I started my trip to his place in a type of covered cart
which is called a "wagon." This same rustic cart which
the previous day transported a dozen calves or sheep, the
next day would carry to church or a tea party a troupe
of girls dressed in their finest apparel, and as this was
Sunday, I saw several so doing. This day is, in America,
the saddest of the week. In France, after having attended
our religious services, the people are free to enjoy innocent pleasures, which relaxes and cheers them after their

week of good work; the priest who comes from preaching
them the gospel often presides over their gay recreations.
Here, after being enclosed for half a day within four
walls, where one is deafened by the strange music of five
hundred people of different ages and sex singing in different keys and where one is made dizzy by the monotonous tones of a four-hour sermon, one is not permitted
to engage in any kind of diversion other than reading the
Bible. Unfortunate are the ones who did not prepare food
on Saturday; they go hungry on Sunday. One cannot
laugh, or sing, or play, nor even go on horseback or take
a carriage ride; and if you found a hole in your stocking,
it would be a crime to mend it. Who is right or wrong?
There are in the world as many Catholics as Protestants,
hence it is permissible to doubt.

I make no decisions between Geneva and Rome. Those
rustics who are not entirely orthodox find recreation in
sitting on the wooden fences (which here take the place
of our green hedges) with elbows on knees, with chin on
hand, waving to the crows. Upon the road I saw quite
a few, and their immobility made me take them for " Scare-
Crows." I arrived early enough to have time to admire,
before dark, the Colonel's pleasing retreat. He has im-
proved it since acquiring it; and American farms unite
certain indigenous qualities that set off the advantages of
the French country houses. From the gallery which sur-
rounds the entire house the eye can stray over the country
seats which border the Delaware, and follow the light
craft, propelled by sail or oar, on their way to Philadelphia.

Among the picturesque sites which abound here, there
is one charming spot from where the lovely countryside
can best be seen. Each day I go for a pilgrimage with
my binoculars; sometimes I take a book and, at times,

I even carry my notebook. Here is the picture of this pleasant retreat:

> In a peaceful and solitary orchard
> Stands the summer house, a perfect sanctuary;
> Two interlaced ash trees, entwined from birth,
> Lend at mid-day their protecting shade.
> The laziest of brooks
> Winds gently through verdant ferns,
> Bathing them in its limpid waters,
> And then passes on beneath a bridge.
> About this quiet place
> The poplar, flexible and straight,
> Lifts its stately trunk;
> And the willow, weeping over cherished sorrows,
> Caresses the luxuriant grass
> With its trailing hair.
> It is there, leisurely sitting,
> I go to admire the countryside,
> Or to build my Castles in Spain
> And dream of all my friends;
> There, also, I go to read your letters
> Which add much to my happiness;
> It is there that my hand writes to you
> The dictates of my heart.

The family of Monsieur de P. is an agreeable and numerous one, which could afford to dispense with outsiders; however, they always are having visitors. Yesterday we had the head of the District Militia and his wife and daughter. The day before I stopped in at their house on my return from hunting and found the Commander, dressed in a denim smock, driving his cart of grain to the barn. His wife, her hair bound in a red kerchief, was vigorously polishing the furniture in the parlor; and Miss Polly, with bare legs and feet, was busy milking the cows.

Yesterday the family was well and tastefully dressed. Miss Polly was as fresh as the flowers she cultivates and as white as the milk which gushes through her fingers; her mother and father conversed well and bantered wittily. They invited our ladies to a "quilting party," and us gentlemen, to a "watermelon frolic."

In case you do not know, people here save all the small pieces of printed cotton that were used for their clothing. When they have accumulated a sufficient amount, they fashion and sew these little pieces together in shapes of stars, rounds, or squares, and they match these colorful patterns upon a white foundation; so, by the end of a year, when they have obtained a sufficient amount for a quilt, they place it upside down upon a quilting-frame and cover it with fluffy raw cotton. Then they make a lining for it from all the old skirts of the family. Thus every thing is ready for a "quilting party."

They enlist all the women within a few miles. Each comes armed with needle and thimble. They encircle the quilting-frame, and while fifty hands sew the counterpane upon the design already traced upon the combed cotton, fifty tongues, mostly agile, discuss the news of the day and the affairs of others. With the coming of night, the hands and tongues rest during the ceremony of tea. I did not learn these details merely for the benefit of my sisters; I hope that before the end of the year they will have a "quilting party" of their own and I, another cover for my bed.

In this part of the country one makes use of every-thing; I might also inform you that any little pieces of old material are cut in strips about the size of one's little finger. These are placed end to end, caught by a thread, and rolled into pound bundles; then the bundles are sent to a weaver, who, for a modest sum, turns them into a good rug for the bedroom. The older the rags, the better the rugs; and it takes two pounds to make an ell. It might also help to know that for these rag rugs, as well as for these quilts, it is permitted to help oneself to the scraps of one's neighbor.

Of the different classes which compose this population, that of the farmer is certainly the most respected. I very much like their customs and manners, to which the Colonel has the good sense to conform in part. He manages all the labor himself; his brothers-in-law take part in the work; and the pretty and sweet Madame de P., her head covered by a large straw hat, gathers the fruits and vegetables which they send to market and gives her attention to the dairy and chicken-house.

At present there are twenty people installed on the farm. Some are mature and others are not. Here is an idea of the life I lead:

Creeping through my window
Each morning, joyous Phoebus
Comes to wake me;
And if the cook is tardy
Preparing our morning meal,
Out I go for a little stroll
Into the fresh and dewy air,
Perfumed with flowers.
After breakfast, each spends a while
With the muses of one's own choice;
Or with the goddess Amphitrite
And Diana, whose kind aid
Adds, at times, to our big soup-kettle.
When dinner is over
Laughing Momus then arrives,

Helping us to enjoy
Light and mirthful banter.
And when the sun's most ardent rays
Begin to plunge into the sea,
We set out to follow its good example;
And later, all refreshed and gay,
We return with song and cheer;
Then, after a supper large and fine,
To bed each one of us does go;
With Morpheus close by our side,
Off we sail to happy dreams.

It is thus that the days run by, with occasional variations because of weather, or light farm tasks, which we all perform with pleasure whenever necessary. You can see that our occupations are many and varied so that boredom is never with us. I am expecting to leave at the end of the week to visit Philadelphia, which is only fifteen miles away. It would be a pity to miss so good an occasion to see the capital of the United States; however, I will not make a long stay. Whatever friends I may find and whatever pleasures I may encounter will not make me forget that I left in New York the person whom I love and admire the most and near whom I pass the sweetest moments of my life.

Philadelphia—August

Here am I in the capital city
Of that vast state founded by Penn;
In cleanliness, no place is its equal,
And they claim to live here very well.
That may be, but certainly
Such is not the case just now!
For yellow-fever at this time

Has entrapped the entire citizenry,
And almost in a second
They depart for other worlds,
Right beneath the doctor's beard.

The city is built pretty much alike in all its parts; so, when one section has been seen, one can dispense with scouring the others; so much so that one cannot find public buildings of a distinguished character or any outstanding monuments; most of the public edifices differ from others only by having a larger number of windows. The houses are all built of brick and upon the same model. The streets are wide, furnished with fine sidewalks, and the houses are aligned. The market is large, clean, and well stocked.

You may imagine, no doubt, that because I am in the capital, I will take occasion to paint for you the manners, the laws, and the customs of the place. Remember that a traveler, like the Wandering Jew, is only passing by and has not the time to make very profound reflections. And also, that I only write to amuse you and divert myself, and I care only to see everything from the pleasant side. Besides—be careful not to show my letters to anyone; people in this country believe they have the right to amuse themselves at the expense of others; but if, by chance, a stranger dares permit himself the least reprisal, then all the population becomes excited, and with fiery eye, cry: " Jealousy, hate, ignorance, ingratitude! " This shows still the perfect hallmark of the English. But Europe is emptying annually so much heterogenous matter into the character of this Nation, that soon it will resemble those stuffed heads of veal that I used to eat often at Beauvilliers—in which there was everything but veal.

More impartial than the Americans, who accord us only

the qualities of being able to make a good rigaudon or
fricassee, I render justice to all who advance themselves
by the advantages which their country offers, and to the
giant strides they make in every thing that goes towards
constituting great empires. I only wish that when each
day they ridicule national pride (in others), they would
not gracelessly terminate their tirade with a pompous
eulogy of themselves. To hear them, their nation is
already the most enlightened and the most powerful in
the universe. The deuce! What airs! Eh, that will come,
I do not doubt! "Each people in turn will govern the
Earth," said Voltaire—but a little patience, if you please!

> One admires a child advanced for his years
> Whose first essay much promise does show,
> But oft as he goes on to mature
> The judgment of men gives his conceit little joy,
> And sarcastic remarks put him back in his place.

It must be said, that if this State is still a child, the
little brat is furiously precocious and can be seen growing
before one's eyes. America rivals us already in many
things. In her big cities, as well as in ours, one finds some
virtues and many vices; some good actions here and there,
and crimes of all kinds; churches and taverns; public
schools and houses for ladies of pleasure; some good
manners and some ridiculous ones; indecency on the first
floor and academies in the garret; luxuries in the midst
of want; elegant fashions next to tatters; and opulence
in carriages by splashing mediocrity on foot.

My candle, in burning to its close, advises me that it
is time to terminate my letter and go to bed. I do not
know if I shall sleep better tonight then I have on preceding ones, the reason being that in this city there is a

type of recurring ghost whom they call a " watchman," who goes about the streets and awakens the people with a screeching voice as he announces the hour and the weather. I cannot see the great utility of this custom, unless it be to fulfil the same purpose as the Turkish criers, who remind good Moslem couples to concern themselves with multiplying the faithful.

> While I, who am yet but young,
> Roundly curse this carillon
> Of hourly walking clocks—
> To begin with, they make me mad;
> For the dragging hours
> That I am far from you
> Seem to me less long in sleep;
> The hateful watchman with heavy step
> Causes me despair by often parting
> The loving son from his good mother—
> Whom a happy dream has brought together.

Philadelphia—August

The final chariots, which resembled the bark of Charon transporting the plague-stricken victims to the gates of Hades, began yesterday their lugubrious voyages. At the sad sight, you could have seen faces lengthened and pale with consternation. Some came and went, packed their bags, rubbed themselves with alkali, sniffed vinegar, filled their pockets with camphor, purged themselves twice a day; some got drunk in order to avoid the most difficult part of death—that of having to face it.

The city emptied itself into the country; one would have thought it a place taken in battle. All the ties of nature, of love, and of friendship were broken; even interest in these matters was forgotten. With yellow

fever one was certain to perish within three days, without
care or consolation, and happy if the hearse did not carry
him off before his last breath. The doctor, when fearless
enough to visit you, has only the appearance of coming
to see you to inquire, as in the comedy: " Where, Sir,
would you like to be buried? " He takes your pulse trem-
blingly and is in haste to pronounce your early death, so
as not to expose himself by seeing you again; and, like
the Trappist monks, you can have here the satisfaction
of admiring your coffin before being ready to occupy it.

In several days there will remain here only the poor,
the robbers, and the refugees from Saint Domingue. The
poor have not the price to pay to escape into the country;
the thieves hope to profit by the absence of the property
owners by despoiling their homes:

> And my dear exiled compatriot,
> Who in this impure desert stays
> And marches with his head held high,
> Does so, poor devil, for believing
> That, having survived a more tragic fate
> Of murder, pillage, fire, and want,
> Heaven in balanced justice now
> Will spare him from the plague.

In spite of this belief, which has so far proved true
for me, I would have left yesterday morning, if I had
not been detained by a tempting invitation to attend a
delightful party. Now you know my weakness; I have
never been able to resist those things, and I have sometimes braved death for less than the supper which I
attended last night.

About twenty young Frenchmen, in order to console
themselves for their sorrows, and to pass the time, have
formed here a type of Song and Poetry Society, which

assembles once a week; I spent with them a most agreeable evening. First, I was introduced into an elegantly furnished room, in which was a large table laid with a delicious cold supper. All the guests gathered about, and the master of ceremonies covered a salt-cellar with a napkin, beneath which each member passed his hand. The president then gravely lifted the napkin, and finding the salt-cellar intact, declared that I was unanimously accepted as an honored member of the society. All at once, they sang in chorus my reception, and the leader of our joyous band signed my diploma with these impromptu words:

> We, the president of these jolly fellows,
> Certify that this said brother
> Seems enough of a " bon vivant "
> To become one of our members;
> And that he can from this time on,
> Together with us, sing, drink, and laugh,
> Sleep, rhyme, or say no word—
> But, naturally, only when his dues are paid.

At last we sat down at table. The repast, prepared by an artist of great merit, was further seasoned with thousands of puns, pleasantries, and epigrams; but dessert brought more serious things. I heard a very instructive dissertation on American " beefsteak " in opposition to French grillards, a profound discourse on the different effects of Madeira and Claret, and a poem on the origin of fricassees, besides a touching elegy on the lack of truffles in the United States.

As for myself, I showed them how much I had profited by my travels by giving the company the proper recipes for " plum-puddings " and " buck-wheat " cakes, and to show my erudition, I proved clearly that it was to Queen Semiramis that we owed the usage of shallots. A half

dozen poets then celebrated Bacchus and Love with odes
and songs. You can well imagine that I was forced to
pluck my lyre, and I know you expect an idea of what
I gave.

Before starting supper, the speaker, as is customary,
read the rules of the procedure, from which I learned that
it was required that all new members to be sworn in were
to give an address to the Society. I arose, cleared my
throat three times, and said something like the following:

> My dear friends, my mouth is watering
> At the sight of this fine spread;
> Despite my appetite, alas!
> It is wanted that I touch it not
> Before having made, in verse good or bad,
> My oath and speech, as is the custom.
> I swear then, by the gods I serve;
> I swear now by the many dishes
> From roast to cheese;
> I swear to eat, drink, laugh, and sing
> In a manner I hope will please—
> Sirs, I am worthy, I believe,
> For I eat like four and I know how to drink;
> I leave, as you do, those austere sonnets
> To the boring philosophers,
> And I leave the cold newspapers
> To the eager politicians,
> And I hate, as you do, both thoughtless tongues
> And malicious spirits.
> My dear sirs, I wish with all my heart,
> To rhyme for you a gracious compliment;
> But I freely confess
> That the large meat-pie causes me paralysis;
> For when I have an empty stomach
> I can have no wit at all,

And I see my thirsty Muse
Casting an eye where the wine is cooling.
So permit me, sirs, to give a toast
Which I offer to your good health.

Thus I spoke and you, no doubt, will find that my discourse was not orthodox, but I think it was such as the occasion called for. The guests who know me will not be fooled by those assumed sentiments; they well know that your son must have more serious feelings:

And that the greatest joy my heart can hold
Is to see, to hear, and to embrace my mother.

Princeton—September

The twenty-eighth of last month, at six in the morning, I left Philadelphia, having as traveling companions a half dozen Anabaptists who were going to be baptized at Burlington. I was curious to attend this ceremony, which began an hour after our arrival.

About a hundred little boats filled with people formed a large semi-circle upon the river, while the bank was crowded with spectators. Perched upon a chair, beneath the shade of a parasol held by a neophyte, the minister declaimed in a loud voice an affecting sermon, which was followed by a hymn sung in droning voices by the multitude. He then entered the water waist-high and called the new converts, who came with penitent air and gathered round him. Despite their fervor, the poor devils could not avoid shivering as it had rained the previous day and there now was blowing a strong west wind.

The first person to be regenerated was a woman about thirty years of age. The minister put one hand on her chest, the other at her waist, and pronouncing the accustomed words, bent her over backwards into the water; a young girl of about fourteen succeeded this woman and made the same performance, though with a bit more grace. The unfortunates swallowed at least two pints of water, which they regurgitated a little later; then, gravely leaving the river, they finished their prayers upon the shore. Next came the men's turn; but as the spectacle had by then ceased to interest me, and besides as dinner time was approaching, I betook myself to the home of Madame d'E., and I can assure you that her wine was not at all Anabaptist.

I left the following morning for Trenton, and I could not dispense with making another stop in that city in order to see and embrace again those good friends who had received me so well upon my first trip. I stayed with them for three days and left with regret, I assure you.

The stage came for me at four o'clock in the morning. It was pouring rain and I had to remain standing in it while they loaded my trunk. When I entered the carriage, my soaking wet coat caused confusion, so I took advantage of this to secure more room. The curved brim of my large traveling hat held at least a pint of water; at each jolting of the stage, I sprinkled my companions, who thought the water came from the windows and took great care to stuff them with straw. As for myself, I was obliged to stop off at Princeton to rub camphor on my leg, which I had bruised in a fall. I profit by this catastrophe to scribble you a letter.

Princeton is a pretty little country town. One can see the large college where the students are instructed in the true principles of Liberty, for they rebel, it is said, two or three times a year. In none of the colleges of this country do the students live as they do in France. Here they lodge and eat in the homes of the residents, to the great detriment of their studies, their morals, and their purses. I now have about a dozen in the room next to mine, where they are drinking, laughing, smoking, and cursing like demons, which causes me to feel somewhat in a bad humor; for when I write or think of my mother,

> That sort of acting about me
> Raises my blood and my bile;
> And I admit being angry
> With whoever distracts me
> From my sweetest amusement.

New-Ark—September

The day after my accident I felt in good enough condition to resume my travels and I got to Elizabethton, where I again took shelter with Monsieur T. Notwithstanding all the pleasures which this happy little city offered me, I stayed only a few days.

Yesterday afternoon I arrived in New-Ark. As I was about to remount the stage, I recognized several of my friends who were going to visit the Passaic Falls, several miles from that city. I am too much of an admirer of Nature to have been able to resist the solicitation to accompany them.

The weather was perfect, the road, which follows the course of the river, offered delightful walks, and my companions were full of mirth and gaiety. The Passaic flows gently from the nearby mountains to the town of Paterson. There arrested in its course by higher ground, it forms an angle and precipitates all at once to the bottom of a crevasse which it has scooped out, or which Nature had already prepared. The various rocks, dispersed here and there on the high borders of the river, form a table which projects over the abyss exactly opposite the falls. Lying beneath it, my head hanging over, I could see its depth. The immense sheet of falling water was twenty feet away from me and the deafening noise hurt my ears. My clothes were wet by a mist of vapor which arose from the cataract on which the sun's rays were playing at that moment, forming a beautiful rainbow.

The river falls from a height of over fifty feet; it is broken about twenty times in its descent to the moment when it arrives in a type of basin, where its white foam accumulates and looks like snow. However imposing the spectacle, it is only a miniature compared to the one at Niagara where, they say, an entire river falls from a height of two hundred feet. Upon returning, we stopped at the inn and I took the occasion to order our dinner. While they were preparing it, I presumed to take down from the wall a poor cracked violin and scratched upon it the air of " Yankee Doodle." You should have seen the room instantly fill with all the family, from the mistress to the kitchen maid. They begged me to accompany the daughter of the house in playing a Scotch reel upon the pianoforte. As you must know, in America, to everyone from the Senator to the cobbler, a pianoforte is as indispensable as a china cupboard. They owe this fad in part to the wives of the French emigrants, who, to aid in combating their poverty, offered their services as music teachers. Unfortunately the passion for harmony in this country only extends, as yet, to six or eight months of lessons; but that is sufficient to have the pretext to ornament their parlors with a fine piece of furniture, though they still try to teach the good people that the fine arts are worthless!

The night was not as agreeable as the day. I cannot accustom myself to the habit of burying myself in feathers and always feeling damp no matter what you do, and being unable to turn over without sending all the sheets and covers flying. Not being able to sleep, we had the idea of going to visit the cataract in the moonlight, and the beauty of the spectacle paid us well for the fatigue of the expedition.

We returned to New-Ark for breakfast, where I am now resting while writing to you; and tomorrow I shall be with you, I hope. As intelligent people always learn from traveling over the world, I have learned that men of all countries resemble each other greatly, and due to this profound, and especially, very new observation, I believe quite decidedly that it is not worthwhile that different peoples should dislike and ridicule each other. If we dance a great deal in France, they dance everywhere in America; and this custom is so popular that it seems they may soon dance at funerals, where, up to now, they go to drink and gossip. The only difference in dancing is that we do so on our toes, whereas here they do so on their heels; this is but a distance of seven or eight inches, and I do not believe that such a trifle is a good reason for one of us to abuse the other. We salute people by uncovering our heads; here they shake the hand with the risk of communicating mange: but there is nothing in either practice that should make one people detest the other. We have our little Dandies; they are found here also. Ours sniff snuff, roll their r's, and drink barley water. Here the Bloods and the Bucks smell their cigars, swear easily, and get drunk on punch. For these differences must two nations fight one another, or must we scratch out each other's eyes because we like fricassees and here they prefer beef sirloin?

As for me, henceforth am I so disarmed of my national prejudices that, were it not for those devilish libellers who are paid to injure us each day with so much abusive language (which makes my blood boil), I would renounce hurling the smallest epigram against any people; even against those with coal-black skin, who caused us so inhumanly to abandon our homes.

This fine and philosophical tirade proves to you, I hope, that I have not entirely wasted all my time while on my journeys:

> And what I realize the more,
> Though I thought it all along,
> Is that there are still friends
> Who overlook a lack of wealth;
> But in virtue and tender affection
> My good mother is without rival,
> And nothing in the world can equal
> That which I feel in my heart for her.